CHASING SEMOLINA

Love and the perfect pasta dish.

A memoir by

PIERO MANNO

Photo by Sal Ali
Model: Tiffany Cole.

Printed and bound in Canada by Art Bookbindery

www.ArtBookbindery.com

ISBN 978-0-615-41319-8

To my mother.

This book resulted from a series of vignettes I shared with that special Monday night group of writers—you know who you are—at Elnora King's place, Fresno, California. Special thanks go to my dear friend Howard Hurtt for the title of this book. An additional acknowledgment goes to Mrs. King for encouraging me to keep writing.

———————————

INTRODUCTION

I became the man I am today on a gray December day. I remember perching on the branch of the poplar tree as I munched dried figs and stared out over the red rooftops of my village toward the distant Ionian Sea.

Mama rushed out of the house with a package tucked under her arm. "Come," she called, motioning me to join her in a hurry. What could be so important?

Inside the house, I watched in anticipation as Mama unwrapped a yellow parcel that lay on the battered dinner table. She revealed a pair of new tennis shoes. Happiness swept over me. Uncle Larry from America had sent me my first pair of shoes. I shivered with joy. They couldn't have arrived at a better time, for it was a cold day in southern Italy.

She took them out of the box, dangled each one by its laces, and smiled. The sight and smell of the shoes conjured images of a rich and distant land.

"You know, Mama," I told her, "one day I'm going to go to America."

I was eight years old the day I uttered those words. I'd no idea they would change my life one day, transport me to another world. And what a journey it would be—from Calabrian shepherd boy to successful chef in America.

ONE

Run my own restaurant? Risk my savings? Work countless hours without a day off for who knew how long? Was this really what I wanted to do?

Yes. I knew the answer the moment I asked. Better to live one day like a lion than a hundred as a sheep. Besides, I could feel that this was my moment. A year from now and it all could change. The time had come to step into the water. For I knew this was no endeavor for the meek.

"Why are you making meatballs now?" I asked as I approached Mama inside her modest kitchen, leaning over the counter-top. A glass bowl containing a mixture of ground beef and pork sat on the counter and the morning air sparkled with the scents of fresh garlic, parsley, and Parmigiano. I helped myself to a cup of espresso from the *caffettiera* on the stovetop. Next to the coffeepot, a pan of tomato sauce bubbled on low flame, faint puffs of steam floating from it. The 1991 calendar behind the stove was pocked with red dots from many such simmerings. Drinking coffee amidst these powerful savory aromas seemed almost the wrong thing to do.

Mama reached over the sink and turned on the water. "Thought I might get a head start before this *inferno* kicks in again," she said with a tinge of disappointment rising in her voice, soap bubbles swishing between her palms, her blank eyes staring out the small window. Light streamed in and flooded the sink, Mama's hands.

July in the Central Valley of California had started with a vengeance. By noon the temperature would soar to over a hundred. Not a whisper of air stirred anywhere. The giant cottonwood tree in the backyard cast its cool shadow on a row of tomato vines. A squirrel rushed across the telephone line clenching something in its mouth.

"Well, let's put everything in the fridge. You get to it when we get back, or even tomorrow," I suggested as she dried her hands on a towel.

She waved a dismissive hand, shot me a look that said I should know better than to tell her how to run her kitchen, and shook her head.

Barely over five feet tall, plump, with red dimpled cheeks, Mama was a force to be reckoned with. Her little ocean-blue eyes were alert, as though the world and everyone in it ought to be questioned.

I dipped into the tiny sugar bowl on the table, poured a teaspoon of sugar into my cup, and stirred it. "I'll shave, then we'll go," I mumbled.

My father emerged from the garden wearing his black rubber boots and faded overalls. He stood on the threshold and tipped his yellow straw hat, exposing sweat-plastered

4

strands of black hair. He wiped the back of his hand across his forehead. "*Buon giorno*," he said, his grin revealing short white teeth.

I returned his greeting and gulped down the last of my coffee. Mama said not a word as she finished drying her hands, threaded the towel back into the refrigerator's handle. She was grumpy. A palpable tension hovered in the air. The heat made her irritable, and when she was cross, she was best left alone. Father knew her well enough to keep his mouth shut. And he did. He cocked his head and shot her half a smile, but said not another word. An inch or two taller than Mama, his well-chiseled face unwrinkled, Father didn't seem like a man approaching seventy.

A long silence ensued while Mama covered the ingredients and stowed them in the refrigerator.

Father glanced at his watch, shot her a last expectant look, and when no response came, turned on his heel and returned to weeding between his rows of tomatoes. A much better alternative than to bask in Mama's gloomy aura.

"Stir the sauce once in a while," Mama called to him as we left the house a few minutes later. "And don't forget it."

He was a disaster in the kitchen. He could barely boil an egg. How could she entrust him with her sauce?

On our way out to my ancient Corolla, which I had left parked under the Modesto Ash tree, I noticed Mama was limping. "What's wrong?" I asked.

"Arthritis." She ran her hand down her thigh and grimaced. "*Ma, come vuole Dio.*" Oh well, God's will be done.

She let out a resigned moan and reached for the car door. Mama was in her mid sixties, but she acted old. I should have been used to her moans and groans by then, for I knew this was the partial muffled cry for sympathy that afflicted most grandmothers of her generation. And it was no coincidence that her mother Teresa, my grandmother, had unknowingly blessed her daughter with the same gift. Mama did have a little arthritis in her lower back and hands, confirmed by X-rays, but I think she exaggerated it, perhaps so as not to part with a long-suffering grandmotherly tradition of the old world.

"Why don't you walk, Ma? It will help."

"Yeah, easy for you to say."

"What you mean? Even Dr. Lozano said so."

"Yeah, sure. Talk is easy. Anybody can do it. Besides, I'm always moving. Isn't that walking? Unless I grow wings and levitate, nobody will see me. Which sometimes I wish..." She let her thought hang in midair. Mama often alluded to things over which she had no control. She shook her head in frustration while fumbling to buckle her seatbelt—a task my parents found utterly fastidious and time consuming. She could never find the latch. "Where in hell is it?" she grumbled. I reached over and buckled it for her.

By the time we got to the delicatessen, less than ten minutes' ride, the sky had developed a blue haze and the air had become even more stifling. Mama inspected herself with a quick glance in the rearview mirror and straightened her mint-green blouse. Gripping the door handle, she struggled out of the car, grunting and complaining that the seat was too low. She left behind a faint odor of mothballs. Although she had a modest but selective wardrobe, Mama kept most of her wool clothes sealed in plastic bags fumigated with mothballs. This didn't guarantee immunity to the rest of her clothes, though, and they smelled of that pungent odor that tickles the nostrils.

Sometimes people around her seemed perplexed by her unusual aroma and the way she dressed. She donned skirts, solid-colored blouses which she sewed herself, and low-heeled Italian shoes—several pairs she had brought from Italy. Although my parents had been in America several years, they hadn't lost the old-world sense of *bella figura*. Good impression. Even if their style of dress drew intense scrutiny from strangers, they didn't adapt to the casual and comfortable ways of the new world. The weekly trip to the local market to buy groceries meant a change of costume for both of them, so to speak, while I trailed along in my *miserabile* attire—Mama's words. Torn shorts, T-shirt, and soiled tennis shoes.

Inside the shop, I introduced her to the owner. "My mother," I said, "and business partner."

"Halloo," she said, extending her hand to the man as though English were her native tongue. This was one of the dozen or so words comprising her entire vocabulary. The man reached out absentmindedly as if Mama was the last item on his agenda.

She began to inspect every inch of the store, taking her time, scrutinizing each nook and cranny. The few employees on duty cast furtive glances at her. Then at me. I felt a little jittery and wished Mama would hurry. There was only so much to see. For all the good sense and diplomacy she could muster in most circumstances, sometimes her blatant old-world ways made me uncomfortable. But there wasn't a thing I could say or do unless I wanted to start a row.

When she finished, she approached the table where I sat with the deli owner discussing the possible terms for the business's purchase. Mama put on her bright smile, the fake one she usually offers to strangers. Then she gave me a disappointed gaze, as though this place wouldn't meet her expectations either. And furthermore, I should have had sufficient common sense to realize this on my own, without wasting her time. With a new and diplomatic smile, she tilted her head forward in a conspiratorial fashion and discretely whispered, "Can't you see the kitchen is too small. The floor shot. Don't you have eyes?" The deli owner shifted his weight in his chair, frowning, possibly wondering what she said.

Mama's words struck deep. Anger rose in me like bubbles. I took a sip from the can of soda in my hand hoping to dampen my rising bitterness, then lowered it to the table and told her, in Italian, to tone it down. The man had offered me a good deal, I said. She squared her shoulders and dropped her hands to her sides, her eyes livid.

"Don't you dare talk to me in that tone again," she told me outside, with a gaze that could have incinerated her worst enemy. "Especially in front of strangers."

My nerves tingled. I closed up. I had learned long ago that silence was the best strategy to defuse Mama's wrath. I put the car in gear and drove away. But two blocks later, Mama had a change of heart. She confessed that she liked the place. "You know, I had such a good feeling in there."

It never ceases to amaze me how people's feelings can change so drastically, how complicated and unpredictable humans are. But I welcomed the news. It was exactly what my mind wanted to hear. And like most men, I sought corroboration, not advice.

"And did you notice the address on the door? 5763. It's uneven, just like your birthday."

I hadn't noticed. I never believed in all that superstitious stuff, her old ways.

"That's a sign of good luck, you know," she insisted.

I stifled a laugh. "Well, Mama, we can always use some of that."

MEATBALLS

Serves 6-8

1 lb beef ground chuck and ½ lb ground pork, or half pork and half chuck	1 teaspoon salt
	10 oz grated Pecorino Romano
3 tablespoons fresh minced flat-leaf parsley	10 tablespoons pure breadcrumbs
4 teaspoons minced garlic	4 eggs 1 tablespoon dry fennel seeds

In a medium-size bowl add meat, salt, parsley, garlic, cheese, and fennel. Place breadcrumbs on a large plate, sprinkle with cold water, barely enough to blend together (do not soak). Add this to the meat mixture, along with 4 eggs. Blend well by hand until incorporated. Taste for salt. Scoop one oz or so of meat into the palm of your left hand, then shape it into a ball with your cupped right hand. Set each meatball on a plate and refrigerate until tomato sauce is ready.

SAUCE FOR MEATBALLS

28 oz diced or plum tomatoes, or San Marzano if available

½ white onion, finely chopped

1 tablespoon olive oil

40 oz water

Salt to taste

Puree tomatoes in blender.

In a medium-sized tall pan add oil, cook onion until translucent, add tomatoes, salt to taste. Cook on medium to low heat until sauce has reduced to a medium-thick consistency, about 15 to 20 minutes. Add water and let it boil. Taste for salt. Add meatballs one at the time and cook with lid ajar over medium heat, about 40 minutes. Extract meatballs delicately with slotted spoon so that they won't crumble. Serve immediately with pasta, or let them cool and serve later, or the next day. Freeze leftovers.

TWO

The transaction concluded, we moved in. I painted the interior a light cream color, and bought used tables and green vinyl chairs. It looked a bit eclectic, but given my budget I had to watch every penny. The purchase of a new refrigerated display case swallowed a major portion of my savings. It was hard to believe the exorbitant prices suppliers were asking for new equipment. I begged for a line of credit all over Fresno. No luck. I looked at the deli's supposedly lucky address and sighed.

I drove to a restaurant auction in Los Angeles to purchase pots, pans, skillets, and other items. Mama went with me, of course. After the auction, I cruised down Hollywood Boulevard, pointing to the movie stars' names engraved in the sidewalks. Her eyes widened like a child in Wonderland's, but she'd only a vague idea of what I was referring to. "I prefer to watch America on television," she said. However, an impulse to stop and give her a little tour seized me. I circled around the neighborhood like a buzzard, but finding a parking space nearby was out of the question. Disappointed, I got on Vine Street instead and headed north on the 101. She didn't mind, she wanted to get home in time to listen to

Angelo Stali's nightly sermons regarding the weather forecast, prepare dinner. She couldn't believe the endless sprawl, the mazes of freeways, and the sea of cars. She admitted the world was too big for her, and couldn't imagine why anyone in their right mind would want to live in such a place when country life was uncomplicated and peaceful.

Mama missed the old country, particularly her village of Pezzolo in southern Italy, where we were born. Most of the time she seemed to be in a state of self-imposed exile, or like a tourist who can't wait to get back to his own country. Everything about her life had a feeling of impermanence. If I bought a piece of furniture for the house, she would reprimand me. "Why you wasting your money? We don't know if we are going to stay here forever." She always referred to us as "we" in the collective sense as though I shouldn't have a mind of my own, and furthermore, mistakenly assuming that I shared her ambivalence about America.

As the San Joaquin Valley emerged into view over the Grapevine, Mama let out a sigh of relief as she unwrapped the sandwiches she had prepared for lunch—she wasn't the type to stop at a restaurant, waste money. She had always told me that the bond with the earth that is made growing up close to the land stays with you forever.

She handed me a sandwich, her eyes sparkling as she admired the endless valley extending before us. It ran on until it merged with the sky, from which the searing California sun beat down. Over the years it had grown on me. Now it was the place I called home.

I bought a used commercial pasta machine extruder from a large caterer and my budget sank lower still. I fretted about whether I would have money left by the time I opened for business. The five years it had taken me to accumulate the savings for this venture flashed through my head. But I tried, as most Americans do, to look at the glass as being half full. Whether anything could be solved with such an attitude was doubtful, but at least it seemed an encouraging philosophy.

One item here, one there, and soon the restaurant began to take shape. But I still had to find the heart of the venture: the stove.

I located one downtown at the farmer's market. The owner, a middle-aged man with wispy gray hair, led me into a dank storage room in back of the center and pointed into a dark corner. There, drenched with grime and buried under piles of used restaurant equipment, sat a once-beautiful commercial stove. As motes of dust floated in slow motion in the bright shaft of sunlight that illuminated the stove, a pang of pain coursed through me. It was a six-burner: big enough. But the grease! God almighty. Some people should have to pass a test before they're allowed to enter the industry. Whoever lets a stove get to that point should be committed to an asylum as far as I am concerned. One can only imagine what such a person might do to the food.

I scratched my neck as I looked at the sad object.

"It's a Wolf," said the man, shining his flashlight on it. The grease glared.

It is true that Wolf stoves are reputedly the workhorses of the trade, but my God, this one was beyond salvation. As I looked at the helpless stove, it dawned on me that time was of the essence. I could not afford to search any further.

"How much?"

"Two fifty."

Too much money for the condition it was in, but worth it. New, they were about eighteen hundred. Plus the damn grease! The first month's free rent the landlord had given me had passed, so now every day gone was money out of my pocket. I'd have to clean it myself. I thrust one hand inside my trouser pocket, fished out a wad of cash, and counted nine twenties while the man shined the light on the bills. "One-eighty cash or I walk," I bluffed, knowing that you never take the first offer, that something is only as valuable as the person who wants it. There was silence for a moment while the man switched the light from one hand to the other. The stove went black for an instant. Then his squeaking voice came again.

"Take it."

It took me a gallon of degreaser and ten hours of scraping to bring the Wolf back to life. When I was done it shined. It was ready to churn out delicacies.

The stove is the instrument with which the cook brings to the table what's inside his head. The soft amber flames respond to the gentle caress of each knob. Just as if he were striking a note on the piano, he feels that music of creativity flow through his fingers, imagines a new creation coming forth from a few ingredients, experiences the visceral pleasure of gripping a skillet by its handle, and then becomes one with his instrument. To me the stove is not an inanimate object sitting on a floor, but an extension of myself: something alive that responds to my command.

I'd trust no one but myself to purchase supplies and raw materials, including the bountiful produce of the San Joaquin Valley. I like to cook what's in season, so buying from major suppliers is the last resort for me. There is pure pleasure in inspecting each item with my hands. I was raised to believe that food isn't like some commodity you slap on a shelf and forget about. Food is alive, breathing. It needs special care and proper handling.

I quit my cooking job in Hanford, twenty miles away, and channeled all my energy into opening my business. I'd planned to open by July tenth, a week away. When I told Mama about it, she said she wanted to anoint the establishment. "Can't open without a benediction. A good cleansing. Want to start off on the wrong foot, or what?" I bit my tongue and said nothing. Cleanse what? The cobwebs of fear and tradition in our own minds, I wanted to say.

Father Negri, who was a personal acquaintance, blessed a bottle of water for the purpose.

On the day before we opened, Mama and I headed to the shop well before the neighboring merchants would arrive to open their shops. I was a nervous wreck. All I needed was to be seen as she went about the anointing and become known as the lunatic with the crazy mother opening shop in town.

The news could spread like fire and bring my business to an early end. As we drove down Fruit Avenue, the paraphernalia necessary for the benediction rattled inside its cardboard box with each bump on the road. Mama stared ahead into the distance, her lips moving silently and the black rosary hanging from her wrist. I tried to recollect if there had been a particular moment in my life when I had completely surrendered my will to her. I shook my head, and couldn't think of anything. Some life I had carved for myself. Some life, *Dio bono*. Good God.

Inside, a faint odor of paint lingered. Mama had picked a vaseful of red and white roses from her garden to scent the air. The place was dim. Light filtered in through the yellow curtains and splashed like a million pearls on the counter. First thing, she ordered me to move tables and chairs away from the walls, and sweep the floor. Then she asked me to leave her alone to get ready for the ritual by reciting a special set of prayers. "If you knew that, why didn't you do it at home?" I snapped, unaware of the procedure's details.

She jerked her head forward, her body anchored to the ground like a pit bull ready to pounce. Her mouth twitched. She glared. "Here, you do it, *sapientone*, know-it all?" She offered me the bowl. I didn't know whether to laugh or scream. I figured I'd better keep quiet. "Just hurry up, will you. We haven't got all day. The merchants are going to show up soon."

"*E, allora*," she said, her voice dripping with sarcasm.

18

So what? I felt anger rise inside my chest. I pushed it back down, aware of the trouble it could cause. Why me, God?

"*Si, si, cammina, cammina, scemo.*" Walk, walk, dummy. She shooed me toward the door like a stray cat. I stepped out and shuffled down the sidewalk to have a cigarette away from her sight. A grown man, and I wasn't allowed to smoke in her presence. Sometimes she treated me like I was still five years old.

People walked in and out of the nearby Food Land market on the southwest corner of Bullard and Palm—an established upper-middle-class neighborhood. A few of them stared at my white chef's jacket. The town had grown during the years I had been gone. I hardly knew anyone among the new faces. Fresno wasn't the small town from my school days any longer. Yet it wasn't crowded nor urban. But growth seemed to be everywhere. Over the next few years it would become a sprawling community, losing that small town charm it once had. However, with its warm climate, rolling hills, paradises of fig orchards, and the endless vineyards outside the city limits, it reminded me of southern Italy. How much more Mediterranean could it get? I thought, feeling right at home. The sea being two long hours away was the only downside.

But today the heat rose from the pavement. I could look forward to another day of searing heat. These were the few times I wondered about my choice of town.

After my smoke, which calmed my nerves a little, I returned to find Mama kneeling on the bare floor, hands clasped, head resting on the counter, still reciting prayers. I had an impulse to tell her to stop all that nonsense. Luckily for me, such words never came out.

Having finished or sensing my presence, Mama struggled to her feet and sighed deeply. She reached into the box, extracted a votive candle, a small wooden crucifix, the holy water bottle, a tiny bottle of oil, and a bowl. Then she spread a white linen cloth over the counter, lighted the candle, and set up a miniature altar. I trudged back to the kitchen so as not to disturb her, but I couldn't help peeking through the door. It was sort of fascinating to watch her. She poured the holy water into a white ceramic bowl, dipped her thumb in oil, and made the sign of the cross above it three times, while her lips recited silent payers. I'd no doubt she was invoking the Lord to my benefit, supplicating the saints, particularly Saint Anthony, the patron of my village of birth, to come to my rescue. Meanwhile, my rational mind knocked at the door of doubt.

She began at once. She lifted the bowl toward the ceiling between her cupped hands, her eyes fixed heavenward. "Oh, evil spirits of this world and the next. I order you to leave these premises so that my son can prosper here from now on. I drive you out, *in nomini Patris et Filius et Spiritu Sancti*, never to return again. And please, Father Almighty, one more request; do not allow any evil to enter this door, for my son's protection. I ask you these blessings in the name of your Son, the most holy Jesus." Then she turned on her heel with the self-confidence of a high priestess performing a sacrosanct ritual.

I watched as she moved her plump body around, whispering prayers, making the sign of the cross, dipping her fingertips into the white ceramic bowl, and sprinkling the mixture of oil and holy water along the walls and in each corner.

Why do I always give in to her wishes? We should have done this at night with no one around. What if somebody sees her?

"Wait," I hollered as she approached the door. I had forgotten to lock it. All I needed was for someone to walk inside and see us.

You know, I walked into this place to get a sandwich and guess what I saw?

The imagined words rang and tumbled in my head like the clapper of a church bell.

After an eternity, she finished. Or so I thought. She told me to unlock the door so she could anoint the outside.

Was she out of her mind? Oh, God, rescue me now. Couldn't she have done this part first? I'd no idea it was necessary, and told her so. She tilted back her head and gave me her icy look. Her chin tightened. I should have known better than to insist and waste even more precious time.

I unlocked the door, told her to hurry up, and set off to wash the sidewalk with a hose as a decoy, trying to shield her at the same time.

Soon, the elderly Armenian couple who owned the jewelry shop a few doors down pulled up in their yellow Celica. I nudged Mama with one elbow and whispered for her to stop. We waved at them.

They returned our greeting and smiled. Good. Nice people. Mama stood motionless next to me, the little bowl clutched to her side, a forced smile across her face.

"*Sbrigati*. It's getting late, Mama," I pleaded. "See? People are showing up."

She hobbled to the front door and sprinkled the last drops on it. I placed a hand on her back to push her gently inside. She turned and gave me a blazing stare. It was a familiar look, one she used to give me as a child, just before she beat me.

"You better watch your step," she said, "and don't think you are too old to get it, because you are not."

Sometimes Mama could be tough as leather, unyielding and unmoving, and like most Calabrians, she meant every word she said. Once in Calabria she confronted a man twice her height over some disagreement. I still remember her words. "You're lucky I'm a woman, otherwise I'd teach you a lesson right now," she had said, standing firm before the man like a rock, her index finger pointing at his taut face as he towered over her, his eyes cold like a rattlesnake's.

Mama had insisted on Wednesday as the opening day. Tuesdays and Fridays were unlucky days to open a business, she said. I told her if people in this country believed all this nonsense there would be no business opening on any day. She sneered, was about to say something, but changed her mind.

The next morning we drove to the downtown market on Merced Street. As usual, it was packed. Shoppers, many of them Russian Armenians, congregated elbow-to-elbow and jabbered happily in their language. Under the faded green tarpaulin covering the stall, Mama helped me select the best produce on display. Oftentimes she would strike up a conversation in Italian with the shopper next to her, marveling at the reasonable prices and the quality of the produce, oblivious to the fact that neither understood the other.

Shopping with Mama was stressful. She liked to take her time to examine each zucchini, eggplant, bell pepper… for blemishes or other imperfections, countless times. She chastised me for moving too fast in selecting the vegetables. She never failed to remind me that she had taken her time giving birth to me. Why couldn't I slow down? Why couldn't I be patient and do things calmly like normal people? She didn't know that years of restaurant work had set my body thermostat on high gear, running all the time, worrying how lunch or dinner would turn out, knowing that everything had to be set and ready, that people usually had an hour for lunch and couldn't wait. And if they did wait too long, they'd probably never come back. Mama knew nothing of the nature of this business. And I doubted she'd ever understand that if you got behind on that line at rush hour, you were dead. The onslaught of orders would run you over, bury you like an avalanche. She had no idea that being a cook is like being a warrior, a mercenary fighting against an invisible and elusive enemy: time.

I looked at the helpless vegetables sprawled on the counter—an array of stunning colors. Poor devils! They were stuck. They had no choice but to succumb to Mama's meticulous and prodding fingers until she welcomed or rejected them according to their good deeds or sins. I suspect that Mama enjoyed playing God every week at the pearly gates of the market.

The day was bright. The heat was slowly descending from under the dome of the blue sky. In a few hours the sun would feel like a branding iron. Mama's upper lip was damp with a thin moustache of perspiration, her high forehead coated with glistening beads of sweat, her eyes fixed on the produce with discriminating purpose.

This end of town seemed abandoned, except for this open-air market, the business district, the inconspicuous industrial sector, and the J&E restaurant supply company down the street on Van Ness. The city's new northward growth had left this portion of town behind like an orphan.

This always made me sad.

This little market seemed so helpless compared with the ones in Milano that stretched for blocks with a river of swaying heads pouring down the middle. I tried to recall the sharp smell of Gorgonzola, the fresh fish, and the sweetness of blood oranges. But Mama came into my head, haggling with a merchant over the price of a piece of fabric for a dress. And now, decades later, she was abiding by the same principle. Pinching pennies. Occasionally I used to catch her staring into a shop's window at a skirt, a blouse, perhaps a dress. But she never bought anything. It was out of her reach. Beyond her means. She consoled herself by indulging in such short-lived reveries. This had been a way of life for her: always alert for bargains, sometimes walking ten blocks to save five pennies. Not to mention sewing our clothes, patching socks and trousers until I was embarrassed to go to school with all those mismatched emblems running down my legs like a mosaic. It made my blood boil with frustration now, thinking that I hadn't become successful, if only to ease her mind of this misery which had consumed her over time. I wanted to succeed at this venture only to avenge that misery, if nothing more.

We loaded the trunk of my car with tangy arugula; luscious, sensual Italian parsley; dandelion; meaty red and yellow bell peppers; tender zucchini; and two cases of shiny purple Japanese eggplant. Although she and Father grew plenty in the garden, Mama didn't seem to ever get tired of them. True, she ended up pickling several cases during the summer.

By the time we left Kamimoto Farms on the west side of the Valley with three cases of blood-red tomatoes, a twenty-five pound sack of sweet red onions, and a case of sweet Italian peppers, we could barely shut the trunk of the car.

"You expecting that many people tomorrow?" Mama asked in a small voice. I knew she worried that I'd sunk my life savings into this venture. She and my father had tried to dissuade me from striking out on my own. The hard experiences of their lives had given them a perpetual sense of impending doom. But had I not taken this chance at starting my own restaurant, I could never have forgiven myself.

I nodded. "*Certo*: why not?" I muttered, my eyes fleeing hers for the serene refuge of the clear Sierra Nevada Mountains in the far distance.

That night I did something I hadn't done in a very long time. I knelt by my bedside and asked the picture of the bearded Lord above my bed to help me succeed at this endeavor—not as much for my sake as for Mama's.

I lay in bed unable to sleep, tossing, thinking, just as men are said to do on the eve of battle. Then I turned to my savior of the night: a book. But I couldn't focus, let alone read. I was taking a big leap. I hoped I wouldn't land flat on my back, go skidding down the road of failure. I listened to the creaking sound of the house settling after a day of intense heat, the crickets chirping outside in the dark, the daunting stillness of silence. And finally, the beating of my own heart. My eyes fixed on a slice of the ceiling bathed in the silver glow of moonlight filtering in through the drapes, and under its magic spell I closed my eyes.

I dreamt I was back in Calabria picking grapes with Mama. There were older women and men I didn't know in the vineyard on the hillside overlooking the sea. I floated through a blur of unfamiliar faces searching for my father. But there was no sign of him anywhere. And as we went about the harvest, wicker baskets and small hook knives in hand, everyone hummed the *Calabrisella* song in perfect unison. The vines bent under the weight of huge clusters of pale green grapes.

PANINO DELLA MAMMA

MAMA'S PANINO

Serves 2

3/4 golden baguette

8 slices of prosciutto

1 oz olive oil

*6 wedges of Parmigiano
¼ inch thick*

6-7 Slices of tomato

A pinch of oregano

Slice baguette in half. Damp/brush it with oil on both sides. A touch of oregano.

Add the prosciutto, cheese, and tomato. Press closed with other half of bread. Slice in half.

THREE

I arose at four-thirty the next morning, dressed, stepped outside, and locked the door. The early morning air tasted fresh and soft. It was so quiet I could hear the crunching of my feet on the cement walk, and so dark, the trees flanking the street were black shadows. My body not fully awake yet, I shivered as I unlocked the car. Dawn was spreading across the gray sky. Up high, masses of fluffy clouds gathered and whirled and floated about as if moved by invisible hands.

Both my parents had asked me to wake them so that they could ride with me to help with the setup at the restaurant for the big day ahead. But Mama and I had prepared sauces and prepped most items ahead of time. And frankly, I liked to work alone, quick and efficient, knowing exactly what had to be done to get the line ready, fill the display case, make pasta, and the rest of the million little things that go into opening a diner every morning. I'd done it for so long, I enjoyed the process, undisturbed.

The clouds had cleared a bit and there was an unmistakable sheen to the washed-out sky. But the air was becoming heavy, announcing a day of heat and sunshine. The palm trees along Fig Garden were still and weary with sleep.

Milano came to mind, where my uncle Frank and I used to get up early on winter weekends to go to his butcher shop. I remembered sitting behind him on his Vespa, one hand curled around his waist as we skidded along in the knee-high blanket of fresh snow. All was calm, all peaceful, the city still asleep. The rooftops and gardens were a spotless white carpet. The naked trees reached out like imploring hands. The landscape was such a shimmering, dazzling white it hurt my eyes. Often the tires slipped and spun trying to cut a path through the thick layer of snow. Sometimes we crashed, falling flat on our backs. The scooter would topple onto its side, the motor revving in the dimensionless glare. Then we stared at each other and laughed until tears ran down our faces.

It seemed a long time ago now. And after more than two decades living in America I wondered where that part of me, and the life I knew then, had gone.

The restaurant was cozy and welcoming early in the morning. A good feeling came over me as I unlocked the front door and stepped inside. I stood there in the dark savoring the moment, watching the faint outlines of the fat palm trees that flanked the side street. The aroma of a batch of meat sauce we had made lingered in the air. The humming of the display case's compressor droned steadily like a legion of bees. A strong sense of pleasure and belonging resided within these walls. As though the little place had been custom made for me. Perhaps it had. I felt proud of what I'd accomplished so far on my own. With no bank loan. No investors to look over my shoulders, breathe down my neck. Through strength of will, perseverance, and faith in my abilities I could make my dream a reality, I knew. I laughed aloud at my own silent monologue. The echo startled the silence.

I told myself I should laugh more.

"Morning, sir," I saluted the little plaster chef sitting on the miniature mint-colored chair by the pasta machine behind the counter. Mama had dressed him in full chef's attire with her seamstress hands. White chef's hat and jacket, checkered chef's pants which seemed to glow in the darkness—he was ready to cook up a storm on the tiny table in front of him. Eggshells and semolina heaped inside a ceramic soup bowl, a wooden spoon in each of his tiny sausage-fingered hands, he stood ready and eager to show the world how pasta was born.

I stepped across the square linoleum floor into the kitchen, my outstretched hands cutting a path through pitch darkness, in the direction of the light switch on the back wall. When I turned it on, the kitchen leapt into being under the brilliance of the fluorescent lights. It was a frugal, tight, and cozy little kitchen with great aspirations and no assets to back up its dreams. It had no glossy stainless steel look to it. No broiler. No griddle or grill. No convection oven. No deep fryer. The latter I wouldn't miss, except to cook *calamari fritti*. And lastly, the kitchen had no heat lamps to keep the food warm. The poor thing simply couldn't squeeze another inch. This meant I'd have to sauté everything, work faster than usual, and dish up the orders all at once so that they would get to the table piping hot, as they should. The worst thing in the world is to serve lukewarm food.

Hell, this was no kitchen…Oh well, too late to worry now.

The deep wooden shelf above the back door brimmed with merchandise. Packets of Arborio rice, cans of black olives, gallons of oil, charming slender cans of imported baby clams, and other items. I had purchased most of these from a single supplier in Sacramento—it has always been my business practice to support local enterprises and not the corporate structure. But in my excitement and wild visions of lines of customers at the door, I had overbought. The confirmations of my grave miscalculations were on the shelf staring at me now. "If you think you're going to get rid of us in a week, you better think again, dear friend. We have settled in this cozy spot and will fight to our death before surrendering our stronghold," they seemed to be saying in a mocking chorus.

The stove I'd resurrected now stood under a six-foot galvanized hood, resting, but ready to obey to my commands. I ran my fingertips along the shiny metal lip on the front, feeling its cool, smooth surface, with the same tenderness with which you'd caress a lover. A feeling of profound satisfaction came over me. My hands itched to handle the skillets, my eyes to observe how well the flames would respond. A deep bond flowed between the stove and me. This would be my little world now. Everything in my life would revolve around this venture. It would demand every ounce of my creativity and care, not to mention hard work, which I was ready to put in. This was my chance to prove to myself what I was made of.

If this business succeeded, I could use it as a prototype for expansion. I'd bring in investors and set up multiple locations. Perhaps I'd even franchise it. The Valley was still a good market, not saturated with competition. It would be perfect for my concept: small spaces, quality, and value. This had been my thinking all along. But I'd better concentrate on the task at hand.

I made myself a cappuccino, awakened the dormant morning air with Pavarotti's powerful melodies, slipped into my Birkenstock shoes, and tied a white apron string around my slender middle, over my shorts. Then I reached under the packets of rice on the shelf and brought out the gray linen sack with $150 in change for the register. "This can be the start of an empire if you play your cards right," my conscience whispered. I luxuriated in the conventional wisdom that all big things have small beginnings, and that money makes money.

I pressed the "no sale" key on the register and laid the money inside the till. The twenties, tens, fives, and one dollar bills settled into their proper slots. And in the front of the cash drawer, I deposited the pennies, nickels, dimes, and quarters in each of its metal pockets. I stood staring at the money. Such an alluring but unconscionable commodity which most men's actions are focused on, hopes and dreams are built upon, the root cause of most ills, and the axis upon which the world seems to revolve. Money—it lay there seductively innocent.

On the wooden table, with my open palms, I pounded and flattened the cold and resistant dough to make focaccia, laid it out on lightly oiled sheet pans, and stacked them in the proofer to rise. In my zeal to impress prospective customers, I'd decided to fill the entire top shelf of the display case with appetizers. People had to take notice of the new kid in town. My kitchen creativity was the only advertising I could afford, and ultimately the best: word of mouth, you might say.

I prepared caramelized pearl onions, eggplant *caponata*, mixed grilled vegetables, and a half dozen more appetizers.

Then I began to get the line ready, the *mise-en-place*, as the French call it. I sliced button mushrooms, chopped scallions, prepared parsley *chiffonade*, and diced tomatoes *cuncassè*.

Around seven thirty the fish order arrived from Morro Bay. I cleaned the New Zealand mussels and cockles, and began filleting a whole salmon. What a beautiful fish is the king salmon. Slick, supple, with that silvery mantle of a skin. I felt almost guilty dismembering it as my knife glided along its spine, smooth like cutting through water. I diced a pound of it into six-ounce portions to set aside for one of the specials.

Once the focaccia had proofed, I oiled it, punctured the puffed-up dough with a fork, and sprinkled fresh sprigs of rosemary on it. Now the aroma seeped out of the stove's oven and floated in the air. There is nothing better than the rich fragrance of baking bread. Once it was ready, I'd finish it with several brushes of macerated fresh garlic suspended in olive oil.

This was it. I was ready to face the great challenge ahead. Ready to start the journey. I thought of the dictum, "Be brave and mighty forces will come to your aid"—or something like that.

Outside in the back lot, I had a quick smoke, waving at Dawn, the jeweler, when she opened her back door. She and her husband were the only people in the center who deigned to acknowledge us, encourage me. "Gudmorning, Piaro. Redi for big day?" She smiled, her sweet and sincere smile.

By the time Mama arrived with my sister-in-law Carolyn, there was a stunning array of appetizers gleaming under the lights of the display case. Roasted yellow and red peppers drizzled with oil and sprinkled with minced basil and garlic, *calamari* vinaigrette, white bean salad, sun-dried tomato *carpaccio*, *pancetta*, more. "That looks very nice." Carolyn smiled, her pleasing blue eyes inspecting the merchandise. Mama said nothing, and strode to the kitchen. Pleasure reverberated through me as I admired the colorful sight. Readying the sandwich station was all that remained to do.

My father had come along, but more out of curiosity. He was not kitchen material. He went outside to inspect the back parking lot, the building's fading yellow walls, and the dumpster, and returned complaining that the grounds weren't swept properly. His statement reflected his obsessive state of mind when it came to cleanliness. "Here." I handed him a push-broom. "Go ahead and sweep it."

He looked at me and frowned. "You mean the whole thing?" He surveyed the lot.

"Sure. Why not? We've got all day."

Warm already, I sipped a bottle of Pellegrino and told Mama about my dream while she fitted into a long green apron.

"The grapes represent money," she said, beaming as she knotted the strings behind her full middle. Mama believed dreams always meant something. I rolled my eyes and wondered how much truth dreams could foretell. But I knew her predictions often proved eerily accurate. For my own sanity I hoped she was right. I was almost forty and my life seemed to be passing far too quickly. My chestnut hair was thinning and graying, and insidious tiny lines sprouted like roots from the corners of my eyes.

I opened for business at ten minutes to eleven. My sister-in-law, Mama, and I looked at each other as if we were embarking on uncharted waters. This was the moment for which I had been waiting for so long. Doubt surfaced for an instant, remembering that my savings had dwindled to almost nothing, fearing that if I failed, I didn't know if I could start over again. A phrase from a sentimental baseball movie had become my mantra: *If you build it, they will come.* After working in countless restaurants, I relished the chance to be my own boss, cook what I wanted. I longed for that phrase to come true, to prove to myself that I could stand on my own feet.

And make Mama proud.

Most people who start a small restaurant remember their first customer. For me the mere sight of the first patron about to enter the premises, as my heart beat with fast wings, conjured up the most thrilling image of eventual financial freedom—the first glimpse of the possibility of achieving the American dream.

The door slowly swung open and an elderly lady made her way into the dining room, walking with a great deal of movement. She wore a flowery burgundy summer dress with rimmed short sleeves. I greeted her, but she didn't seem to hear me. She stopped, baffled, her eyes surveying the tables. She shot me a quick and polite smile with a slight upturn of her mouth. "Hon, where do you want me to sit?" she asked, her voice warm, almost grandmotherly.

"Anywhere. You've got the place all to yourself today."

She leaned forward and reached for the closest chair, eased herself into it with a satisfied sigh. Then she peeled off one of her black shoes and propped her left leg up on a chair. "I was wondering when in the heck you were going to open up," she said, craning her neck in my direction.

I explained my situation to her. We made small talk. Then I asked her what she would like to order.

"What you suggest?"

I made her fettuccine with tomato and basil. She told me a little about her life, and her beloved city of San Francisco.

Then as she was about to leave, I noticed that she'd hardly eaten anything. I asked what was the matter. "Oh, nothing, hon. Just wanted to come in and see what you and the place looked like. Had a sandwich an hour ago."

I walked her to the door, and opened it for her. She turned on the threshold. "You will do just fine. Anybody that uses fresh basil in his tomato sauce knows what they are doing." She handed me a ten dollar bill—my first sale. "This is for good luck." She waved goodbye.

Elenora, my adopted American grandmother.

Soon people began trickling in, wandering around aimlessly. As I greeted them from behind the counter, I pointed to the specials board on the wall, reciting each one with fervor, hoping to make a sale. Mama and my sister-in-law stood in the kitchen as reinforcement, watching, waiting. A few customers of the previous owner's stumbled in, gaping at the changeover, inquiring about his whereabouts, inspecting the long list of specials as though they were examining some obscure document. A stout older woman turned to me and asked, "So, this place is Eyetalian now?" Passersby followed, and a few supportive fellow merchants.

But around three o'clock the tiny flurry of activity that had animated us ended. The place fell silent again. Mama glowed with excitement. To her this seemed like a lot of business. But a wretched feeling gripped my chest as I gazed at the appetizers. We'd sold mostly sandwiches and pasta salads. Those few patrons must have looked upon the appetizers as mysterious decorations. My valiant efforts to explain each and offer free samples had been ignored.

My sister-in-law left, and took father home. Mama had told him to go, that he was useless around here.

Some time later, I glanced at the register with dread. When I opened the till, Mama's eyes brightened at the five, ten, and twenty-dollar bills. But the total on the tape visible through the tiny plastic window of the register showed eighty-three dollars and change. I cringed. Mama seemed delighted by this sudden ascension into the realms of wealth. I had no heart to even do the checkout. I slid the drawer shut, flashed a big smile, and walked out the back door, careful not to let her see the sheen of moisture in my eyes. Leaning one hand against the gray chain-link fence by the loading dock, I hung my head like a sad puppy. I lit a cigarette and blew smoke into the air. The sun felt hot on my neck. The sullen Chinese man from the takeout place gave me a quick glance as he carried a bag of garbage to the dumpster. I'd done so much work for nothing. How could I have been so gullible as to think that people in this town knew, much less wanted such foods?

Welcome to the real world, I whispered to myself, and extinguished the cigarette, nearly pulverizing it, by rubbing it against the fence.

But I wasn't going to give up until there was no more hope to hang onto. I'd invested every penny I had, and worked too hard to watch my dream evaporate in the first few hours. I'd use every secret I'd learned working in restaurants on both sides of the Atlantic.

I would succeed.

The specials I'd announced on the board hanging on the wall hadn't fared any better than the appetizers. I was headed down doom's path if I couldn't learn what people were willing to eat around here. Perhaps some of my specials on it were ahead of their time. Risotto with porcini, *pappardelle* with *crimini* mushrooms and salmon... Hardly anyone had so much as looked at them.

Mama fed a few of the merchants next door with some of the excess food. She even approached a rough-looking homeless man with cotton pellets stuck up his nose who slept under the rafters of the supermarket at night, handed him a plateful, and insisted he take it.

When I reprimanded her for taking a chance by approaching a complete stranger, she said the man could have been Jesus.

That left me speechless.

We'd have to eat all the food, or take it to the Poverello house. My brothers, prodigious eaters, could knock off half the appetizers by themselves. Perhaps Silvio could take some to school and break bread with his colleagues.

Despite the encouragement my sister-in-law offered, I couldn't believe I'd gone so far astray in my projections. Mama had warned me that most people probably wouldn't know half of these dishes. Well, she was right. But one thing was clear. I would have to come up with an alternate menu, and quickly. I would offer a large selection of pasta dishes, a few meat dishes, sandwiches, and experiment with daily specials. I even contemplated opening for dinner, accepting that if I did so I'd never again have a weekend off.

I hadn't cooked on the line since I'd left my previous job, and I missed the adrenaline rush that went with it.

Waiting and hoping for another flurry of business to save the day, I went back to the kitchen and diced Roma tomatoes from Father's garden. We were so proud of the contribution he made with his own organic vegetables. I tossed half-handfuls of chopped scallions into a skillet with olive oil, and sautéed a quick tomato and basil sauce to marry with the penne. I noticed a precious glow of happiness in Mama's bottomless eyes—a sort of pleasure I'd never seen before.

At the table, Mama said grace. I bowed my head, listening to her supplicating words. She droned on a little, and by the time she finished the food had gone lukewarm.

She made the sign of the cross.

"*Buon appetito*," she said as she spread a paper napkin across her lap.

I nodded, twirled a forkful of pasta on my spoon, and shoved it into my mouth.

Then I pushed my plate to the side.

"*Che c'e?*" Mama's piercing eyes lingered on me, her face flushed. Age lines were sneaking in around her delicate neck.

"Nothing," I lied, sipping from a glass of water. "I'm not hungry."

"*Sono gli antipasti*, isn't it?" Her eyes stabbed at me and she shot me a teasing smile. "Told you people wouldn't know these plates. But you are such a *testa dura*. Never listen, really

41

listen. Well, look at it this way: at least you don't have to worry about me preparing your lunch for a week."

She was right. I never listened to anyone. Unlike some people who listen for tones and intonations, I hear and record every word spoken to me—or within earshot. But I normally let them bounce off me when nothing interesting captures my fancy. And Mama's sermons were often dull music to my ears. But how could I deny my own stubbornness now? This time my intuition, which had been the great compass of my life, had failed me. I felt humbled and a little reproachful. I remembered Shakespeare's verse, "It's better to have loved and lost, than not to have loved at all." My hopeless romantic nature found solace in those words, knowing that I hadn't been the first fool to give free rein to his impulses and fail.

The air conditioner hummed its steady, buzzing tune as it fought the merciless July heat, reminding me that a portion of the money we had just pulled in was going to help make the utility company a little richer. Before we left, Mama took another votive candle from her purse and lighted it. Then she nailed the crucifix on the wall above the flickering candle. She knelt on the floor, lowered her head, and laced her fingers together. "*Grazie, Madonna Mia*," she began. As I waited, I ached at the thought that we hadn't even covered the day's expenses and tried to brush aside the most burning question whirling in my head: will I make it?

Watching Mama light the candle unleashed a flood of emotions that transported me back in time nearly thirty years.

PENNE AL POMODORO

Serves 4

*This is a simple, quick, and healthy dish that can be prepared in minutes. Whether you have company or need to feed hungry, impatient kids, this will do. You may substitute pasta of your choice. **Please consult the last section of the book. Appendix one and two.***

2 tablespoons extra virgin olive oil	*14 oz diced, ripe tomatoes* *Salt and pepper to taste*
4 oz scallions	*7-8 minced basil leaves*
1 tablespoon garlic cloves, minced	*1 lb Penne Rigate*

Wipe scallions with a damp cloth to remove dirt. Peel outer skins and discard, along with ends of scallions. Dice into half-inch cubes. Use small bowls or ramekins to collect items.

Wash, dry, and dice tomatoes.

Heat oil in a large skillet on medium heat. Add the scallions and cook until they are translucent, 1 to 2 minutes. Add the garlic and stir quickly. (Garlic can burn in less than ten seconds, depending on the heat intensity.) Add tomatoes. Salt to taste. Simmer 3- 4 minutes. If it looks dry add a bit of water from the pot where pasta will be cooking.

When water comes to a full boil, add 1 tablespoon of salt, and the penne. Cover until it reaches a boil again. Remove lid and cook on high heat until pasta is al dente.

Pasta should always be cooked on a high flame.

Drain pasta and transfer into skillet. Toss for about 1 minute, or until pasta has absorbed sauce. Adjust salt and pepper to taste. Sprinkle a free hand of extra virgin olive oil on the pasta as a final coronation. Add minced basil at the last minute. Serve.

Note: Basil must not be washed. This dissipates its flavor and aroma. Wipe each leaf with a clean flannel cloth. Mince it just before using it.

Usually this dish doesn't call for the addition of grated cheese, but if you like it, by all means use it. If you like more sauce, add from marinara (Appendix 2)

There is an old Italian saying: pasta will wait for no one.

FOUR

Southern Italy, 1960s

When I was a boy growing up in Calabria I wanted more out of life than the poverty my family and I shared. I dreamed of living in a house with electricity, indoor plumbing, and running water.

We lived in a small shack built with stones, terra cotta, gravel, and a dirt floor. Most nights I sat on its doorstep counting the stars and dreaming of a better life.

One day that would all change.

It was a quiet spring evening, my favorite time to stare at the distant mountains outlined against a purple and red sky. Every night the same thought returned to me. What world lay beyond that mysterious horizon—beyond the impenetrable chain of mountains that stood tall and still against the sky? The sight always left me breathless, in awe, and determined to one day climb its snow-capped peaks and see what was on the other side. Was there a better world my eyes couldn't see? I'd no clue, but I suspected anywhere must be better than this godforsaken place.

"Pierooo." Mama's voice rang in my ears.

When Mama called, I had better jump. I rushed out of my thoughts, got up, and hurried inside the house, stumbling over the whitewashed steps. "*Si*, Mama."

"Here. Hold your brother while I make something to eat." She handed me the baby.

I sat in a yellow straw-padded chair by the door and cuddled him in my arms. Mama walked to the fireplace in the corner. The house was a dim, square room with a table and four chairs in the middle of it. A large bed sat in a corner where Mama and my two brothers slept. My little bed was tucked against a wall.

We'd curdled goat cheese today, and the sweet smell of whey hung in the air. The flies buzzed, chasing the aroma. My stomach churned and twisted at the thought of another dinner of pasta with ricotta. I grimaced, but was thankful for it. It was better than going to bed hungry, on an empty belly.

I laughed aloud watching my younger brother Silvio fanning fireplace smoke from his eyes. He stomped his feet and complained about our home's lack of windows. The baby kicked and moaned, so I hummed a tune and swung him in my arms to try to quiet him.

Mama tilted her head sideways as she stoked the fire. Her long blond hair spilled to the side, and under the smoke cloud she threw me a knowing glance. I blushed and looked away. This night there was tenderness in her I rarely saw.

"Father is coming tomorrow," she said, and dropped a handful of long, dry pasta into the boiling kettle.

Had I heard her right? "Father is coming?" I yelled above the baby's cries. I could feel my heart racing. I shut my eyes and tried to remember what he looked like. But no picture formed in my head. I was mad at him for leaving me to grow up without a father, for not being there when I needed his presence. I never told Mama about it. She would have scolded me for having such thoughts. So I remained silent. I kept to myself, alone, with my goats, the slingshot and the wind as my company. Gone to Milano for work for months at the time, like many men of our village, Father had become a stranger, always out of my reach, always gone. I learned to depend on myself. But there were times I missed him. Sometimes, when I asked Mama when he'd come home, she'd tell me to look at the moon because it could see where Father was. So if I looked up at it, I could see him too, she'd explain. That's what I was waiting for on the steps, when she called a little while ago. The moon.

"God willing," Mama said, and made the sign of the cross. "Now don't you be mouthing off to anyone till we are sure, you hear me?"

"*Si*, Mama. When is he coming?"

"Tomorrow, he says in his letter. Or maybe the day after. And then he has to walk over an hour from the train station. Who knows what time he will get home."

I had heard about trains, but had never seen one. I tried to picture what one might look like. There was anticipation and excitement in Mama's voice. When I saw happiness in her eyes, my heart swelled with joy. Life should have been like that every day.

Mama was almost always sad. I knew she missed my father, and life without him was tough. But I worked hard to please her. I used to milk the goats in the morning before I went to school—and drink most of the milk at the same time, till Mama found out one morning and smacked me on the back right into the metal pail. I took the goats out to pasture afterwards. I cleaned the chicken coop behind the round brick oven and gathered dry sticks for the firewood that Mama would use to bake bread every week—golden round wheels. And lastly, I tended to my homework every night in the dim light of the kerosene lamp. Mama made sure of that. And while the lamplight's shadow danced on the wall, my brother crawled up my legs like a lizard, begging me with his eyes to lift him into my lap. But no matter how hard I tried to please her, it made no difference to Mama. She rarely smiled. So I kept quiet and hoped that someday my life would change, so that I wouldn't have to be a shepherd forever, because that wasn't what I wanted.

"Why do you want to know?"

"*Niente*, Mama. Nothing." I was hoping to miss school with this excuse, and escape the teacher's punishment when I gave him the wrong answers. I'd get two or three slaps on each of my palms with a wood paddle. Or I'd have to kneel on the cement floor, facing the wall, until my knees went numb.

Before we went to bed, I knelt next to Mama by her bedside and recited prayers. We prayed every night.

I wondered who this mysterious God was, and why I could never see Him. I wondered why He had not saved my old nanny goat from dying in the birthing of her two kids. "Can God really hear us, Mama?"

She raised her head, looked into my eyes, and smiled. "*Dio* can hear and see everything we do from up there." She pointed to a slice of the starry sky that could be seen through the open door. "Don't you ever doubt that."

I listened to her words, doubt buzzing in my ears.

A cool sea breeze blew in through the open door as a confirmation to Mama's words, rustling the leaves of the giant oak tree below the house. I stiffened with fear and scooted closer to her.

Unable to sleep from the excitement, I tossed in bed. I closed my eyes and thought about the city I'd heard so much about. A blur of images formed in my head. They became clear: tall buildings, glowing lights, roads paved with gold, and cars crawling like ants.

In the morning I woke up early as usual. I got ready to make the rounds in the nearby woods to pick up the catch from my traps before I headed to school.

Outside the wind was blowing. Goosebumps formed on my legs—I wore shorts most of the time, shorts sewn by Mama from cloth sent by Aunt Mary in America. The village was quiet. The treetops swayed in the forest below. I stumbled down the steep hillside, my feet plunging ankle-deep into the cool, sandy ground. I grabbed onto pungent-smelling ferns so as not to fall, my hands stained green.

It was eerily dark under the chestnut trees. Beneath the slabs of rock I'd set up the night before lay flattened sparrows, the tiny piece of dry cheese I used for bait dangling from their beaks. The sight always left me sick to my stomach. I wished there was an easier way to catch them. The birds provided most of the meat we ate. Mama cooked hers in tomato sauce. I liked mine roasted on a skewer over red coals.

After school I hopped down the trail home on one foot, then switched to the other, whistling, hoping to find Father home. Down below, in front of the house, Mama was hanging clothes on the line to dry. They flapped in the breeze like kites. The sun was high in the sky. A flock of doves drifted across it.

"Is father home?" I panted when I got to her. I had run the last stretch of the trail.

"Not yet."

"Well, why not?"

"How many times I need to tell you that I don't know?" Mama shifted into her serious tone. "How was school today?"

"All right, I guess." I shrugged and made a circle on the ground with my bare feet. The soil was still moist from the rains that had lasted longer than usual that spring. The hills were dotted with patches of green grass. The patches of snow on the lower slopes of the mountains were slowly melting away. In another two months school would be out. Then the hills would become brown again from another season of scorching heat. Maybe this would be my last spring in Calabria.

Disappointed, I walked into the house. I cut a piece of dried ricotta cheese and a slice from Mama's wheel of bread with my pocket knife and stuffed my pocket with a handful of dried figs. Then I reached under my bed for the slingshot and tucked it inside my waistband. This was my friend, my protector. With it in my possession there was nothing that intimidated me. Uncle Frank had taught me how to use it. The slingshot was a reminder of him trotting me on his bony shoulders, my hands clasped around his neck, uncle playing donkey.

"Careful on that tree," Mama hollered as I stepped out the door.

It was the same old tune. I paid no mind to it.

"Come here," she called in a dry tone as I walked past her.

The first thought that came to mind was that I might have done something wrong and she thought I needed a couple of slaps across the face. But I couldn't think of anything. Not lately. Unless…unless she saw me shooting the donkey's rear with my slingshot when mountain people passed through the village. When she got close, I flinched and raised my hands for cover. But she reached out with her arms, bent down and kissed me on the cheeks. "*Bellu da Mamma*," Mama's dear, she said, pulling me in to her, stroking my hair. I breathed a sigh of relief.

At the shed, I opened the door to let the goats out. I whistled them up the trail, whacking my wooden stick into the ground, and yelled at them not to wander off.

Once I had turned them loose on the flat plot of oak trees near the school ground, I climbed up the poplar tree to my hideout. It was made of two planks of wood across two branches. This was my secret place where I dreamed the dreams of my lonely shepherd life. From there I had a breathtaking view overlooking our entire village: nine houses scattered along a hillside. A gravel road about a kilometer away stretched eastward. To the south the blue Ionian Sea sparkled. Toward the north stood the impenetrable mountains. And in the distance, above the banks of the dry riverbed, sat the yellow church where my parents were married, and where my brothers and I were baptized.

From my hideout I kept watch down the trail. It stretched like a snake through the arid, rolling dunes. Huge limestone boulders crouched along its lonely path. Not a soul could be seen or heard. Silence and stillness covered the land, broken only by the chorus of summer cicadas, or by the chirping of sparrows, the mewling of sheep, the braying of donkeys, or by the howling of the wind that bent the treetops and whipped the fluffy clouds across the clear sky.

Summers were baking hot in our village. So hot that when I stepped on rocks, the soles of my feet burned. Winters were mild, with heavy downpours, and with it came landslides and hordes of snails. Mama would clean the snails in cornmeal and then cook them with tomato sauce. Occasionally I caught sleepy eels idling behind rocks in the damp riverbed, smacked them in the head with a stick, and trudged home with my catch dangled proudly over my shoulder to show to the villagers and Mama. But for the most part, we ate wild vegetables that grew on hill slopes. Chicory, fennel, mushrooms, dandelions, sautéed with garlic and oil—when we had some.

Some days from the hideout I could see Mama out in the distance by the side of a small stream, soaping clothes on rocks, singing with the rest of the women from the village in a sweet chorus that lifted and echoed in the air.

My eyes always turned north beyond the mountains, toward Milano, where Nonna, Uncle Frank, and two aunts had moved when I was five. I dreamed of going there. I wanted to live in a house with modern amenities and not be a shepherd all my life.

As the day wore on, there was not a sign of my father. I pictured him slowly climbing up with a sack of flour on his shoulder when he went to town to buy salt and matches. But the trail remained deserted. I decided to wait for him until dusk. I took out the cheese and bread and munched on it. Light filtered through the leaves and danced on my face as I dangled my feet and kept an eye on the goats below. Then I reached inside a small hole I'd carved in the tree trunk, took out my little bamboo flute, and went about playing it. I'd no ear for music, but I tried to bring out the melodies inside my head. This happened rarely. But the sweet sound of the flute helped me pass the long hours of silence all shepherds must endure.

Dusk was settling, and still there was not a sign of Father. I wondered if something might have happened to him.

I climbed down the tree and headed down the trail to the shed with my four goats. I hurried because I still had to fetch water in a terra cotta jug from a spring at the foot of the mountains. The houses below the trail looked like pale ghosts in the twilight. Ours sat in the middle of a row with three other houses. My grandfather had built it with the savings he earned working in the coal mines of West Virginia. The date was inscribed on the wall next to my little bed, and every night I slid my fingers over the number—1918— and dreamed of a faraway land called America.

I was about to lock up the shed and walk home when out of the corner of my eye I saw something move. I turned around and came face to face with Father. His slicked-back hair, sharp face, and pencil-thin moustache were unmistakable. My heart quickened with excitement. He smiled, showing his even, white teeth, then he moved closer and wrapped me in his arms. I felt the beating of his heart under his shirt and smelled tobacco on his breath. He let go of me, reached inside his jacket pocket, and handed me a chocolate bar.

"Are you ready to go to the city?"

I nodded, so excited I could barely say a word. We walked home together, his hand on my shoulder as the sun sank over the mountains.

That night Father cuddled the baby in one arm and bounced Silvio on his knee with his free hand. Mama was getting dinner ready, talking to Father. She had twisted the neck of a hen to celebrate the occasion.

I sat outside on the doorstep looking at the dark mountains. The moon seemed to smile, knowing my father had come home. His presence made me feel safe, happy. I wasn't mad at him anymore. I kept staring at him when he wasn't looking. I'd the same hook nose, same hazel eyes. How could I have been mad at him? It wasn't his fault he had to leave us. That was our life. But now all that would end. A new life was in store for us. I stared at the houses below in the darkness. Pezzolo. A tiny village of white-walled houses and peaked, red-tiled roofs. A land of sheep, goats, and tired old donkeys. A land of strong women in long black dresses walking barefoot, straight and proud, carrying on their heads water jugs, bushels of corn, or bundles of dry wood.

Above the mountain's rim the sky lit up with a constellation of tiny bright stars, stars that seemed to light the entire sky on fire. There were just too many to count that night. Suddenly, one broke away and fell down the open sky with a tail of fire chasing behind. It had been awhile since I'd seen a falling star, and I knew then it would be the one lighting my path and watching over me.

SPAGHETTI RICOTTA

Serves 4

This is a very filling dish. To me it brings back memories of long-bygone days. The quality of the ricotta is very important. It should have a velvety creamy texture like it does in Italy.

14-16 oz ricotta   **Salt to taste**

1 lb of spaghetti or other pasta of your choice

Pour ricotta into a large skillet and work it into a fine paste with spoon.

Bring a pot of water to a boil. Add 1 tablespoon of salt, and cook pasta as indicated in the previous recipe. Taste and adjust for salt. Always taste food.

Drain pasta, leave it a bit watery, and transfer to skillet. Turn flame to low, mix and coat for 5 seconds. Serve at once.

FIVE

The time to leave arrived. The goats, chickens, what little furniture we had, and the picks and shovels father used to hoe his orchards with were given to Mama's sister-in-law, Enrica.

The last evening before we left, I walked to the shed to bid the animals farewell. The two baby goats hovered close to the shed's half-wall and licked the cube of sugar in my hand. I leaned over and patted them, slid my hand over their smooth backs in the clear moonlight. Tears came to my eyes—I sensed this could be the last time I might see them. They had been so

Me holding the baby, Silvio ready to jam. The goat shed behind my head. The trail to the school ground on the upper right corner.

much part of my life, and I ached at the thought of separating from them. I strode back to the house, sad for leaving part of myself in the village, but happy for the new adventure awaiting us.

I sat on an overturned wheelbarrow under the oak tree in front of the house. Darkness had deepened and under the glow of a full moon, strange and eerie shadows surfaced here and there, like the watchmen of the night. A cool sea breeze swept over the cluster of cottonwood trees below the house. It rustled in the oak leaves, rushed up the hill, and disappeared into the night. I stared one last time at the blackened mountains leaning against the sky. They had given me a bittersweet hope for so long. I'd miss them too.

That night I lay awake in my bed staring at the ceiling. I took deep breaths to calm the excited shaking of my body and ease the feeling of suffocation. This happened to me sometimes. The light of the candle flickering on Mama's dresser illuminated the silver crucifix on the wall, a picture of Saint Anthony, and her black rosary, casting eerie, moving shadows. I slid under the covers and recited a silent prayer so the spell wouldn't last too long. My parents, in their bed with my brothers in the middle, talked long into the night. I wondered how my life would change now. What new friends awaited me in the city.

In this room, Mama had given each of us life. I was the firstborn, next came Silvio, and the baby last. Here I'd heard my brothers' first cries and seen their first smiles and tears. Here I'd observed their tiny mouths sucking from the plastic bottle Mama left me to feed them with when she went to the mill to grind corn. In the tattered crib, I'd watched them stick their curled fingers inside their mouths and moan with a twinkle in their eyes. Then, as they slept, I'd waved a rag to keep the flies away. One overcast day I'd knocked the lighted lamp onto the table with the rag and nearly burned the place down. Between these four walls, watching my brothers breathe, my eyes had opened to the miracle of life. On this floor I'd seen them crawl, then take their first stumbling steps as Mama extended her arms and cheered.

In the morning a wedge of light splashed on the floor and filtered in under the door. A rooster crowed, and soon the dawn chorus was underway.

I fetched the box under my bed containing another pair of tennis shoes Uncle Larry had sent me from America. Mama had warned me not to wear them until now. Sitting at the edge of my bed, I quietly took them out of the box. They were white with a blue band along the sides. I loosened the laces, ran my hand inside their smooth linings, then stepped inside. They felt soft and comfortable, my calloused feet snug and protected. I tied the laces, stood up, and took a few steps in place. I had to put a hand over my mouth to hold back a rising giggle.

Once ready, we stepped outside. It was a crisp spring morning. The sun was just over the sea. And judging from its height in the sky, I guessed it was about nine o'clock. A few families had gathered. Toothless older men, barefooted kids in patched-up clothes, and older women wearing long black dresses huddled outside and waited with anxious faces to wish us good-bye.

I kissed men and women on their leathery brown cheeks. I shook their calloused hands as they patted me on my back, mumbling that luck had chosen us and, as usual, chosen to leave them behind. My heart went out to those deep-lined faces, those hopeless eyes heavy with fatigue.

We started up the trail that led to the school grounds, a sad chorus of farewells echoing behind us. Father carried a warped black suitcase on his shoulder. I swung the wicker basket in which Mama had put a wheel of bread, olives, dry ricotta, raw almonds, and two bottles of wine for our journey. Mama carried the baby pressed to her chest. Silvio strolled along, grinning. I'd traded my slingshot for his share of the chocolate and he seemed in seventh heaven. The neighbor's old one-eyed dog followed us at a distance. Sparrows twittered in the oak trees.

When we reached the school, I turned to see part of the red tile rooftop of our house between tangles of swaying branches before it disappeared. Then I gazed out in all directions: at the river, the church, the little cemetery next to it, and the snow-capped mountains in the distance. I promised myself I would carry those images with me everywhere I went until the day I couldn't remember them anymore.

Father, in the meantime, had walked to the edge of a cliff, and stood with the suitcase at his feet, his *beretta* in hand, staring at the cemetery. We paused. The grandparents I had never known were buried there. I wondered where my parents would be buried one day. The thought sent chills of fear up my spine, left me trembling and terrified.

The baby gave a short cry. Mama rocked him in her arms and hummed a soothing tune. Silvio kicked the ground with the tip of his shoe. Purple dust rose into the air. The braying of Aunt's donkey echoed off the mountains and traveled across the valley. Father stood motionless, a sad look in his eyes. We waited in silence for him. I looked at his bruised and calloused hands. After all his trips to Milano and all of Mama's worries and sleepless nights, it pained me to think his life's account amounted to nothing more than a battered suitcase and four hungry mouths.

He made the sign of the cross, adjusted the hat over his head, and joined us again.

We caught the trail down through the thick patch of olive trees and prickly pears below the schoolhouse, then headed down the motor road. Standing on the shoulder of the trail, Father snatched a twig from an olive tree, bent it into a U, placed it inside the left pocket of his jacket, and patted his chest.

Papa had ordered a car to take us to the train station in the town of Caulonia. I'd seen a car only once before, when Mama's cousin David came to visit us from America. I'd been shocked for the entire day by the spattering noise made by the strange object rolling down the road. When my goats heard it coming, they raised their heads. Their floppy ears stiffened, and when they saw it approaching, they took off running.

When we arrived, on foot, at the motor road, I saw the car. It was waiting for us. The driver, a stocky, red-faced man with eyes like an owl, motioned for us to climb in. The green Fiat lurched ahead, crushing gravel under its tires. I turned and peered through the rear window. White dust rose behind as the car sped down the road. Above, I saw the dog waving its tail and barking. Then I spotted the tip of the poplar tree that had been my hideout. The mountains beyond it stood smiling. I tried to choke back my tears, but they spilled down my cheeks. These were tears shed for leaving behind the only world I knew.

About half an hour later, we entered a small brick railway station and sat on a wood bench. I remember the morning sun beating on the tracks and the calm breathing of the sea a couple hundred meters away on the other side of the tracks, beyond the marshes. The smell of salt drifted to me. It was the first time I had seen the sea from up close. It was so big, it took my breath away.

We waited, and waited, and waited for the train. I fell asleep.

It was deep into the night when we got to Rome. I pulled down the train car's window, leaned my head out, and peered into the misty and almost deserted station.

We gathered our things, got off, and sat on a cool marble bench alongside one of the platforms. What a surprise it was to discover that the train looked like an open accordion. But what shocked me most were the electric lights in the station, so glaring and bright they hurt my eyes. In comparison to the kerosene lamp we used at home this seemed like magic. I'd never imagined that anything else produced light besides the sun and the moon.

Mama balanced the baby in her lap to give her arms a rest. Poor Mama looked tired and sick. She'd suffered from motion sickness during the ride and had vomited several times. The baby was sound asleep. He looked so comfortable that I envied him for a moment. Father stood down the platform blowing a cloud of cigarette smoke and staring at the tracks, lost in thought. The station smelled of coffee. Silvio was aiming the slingshot everywhere and finally Mama told him to stop pointing it or she would take it away. He frowned and put it in the back pocket of his trousers, then came over and curled a hand around my neck.

A large clock hung on a wall. I stared at the big circling white hand, wondering what time it could be. Without any sun, there was no way I could tell time, but I knew it was late. The silence of the night was broken only by the echoing voices of maintenance workers who, with lanterns in hand, inspected under and between parked train cars. Then they barked and waved to each other as they found each car all right. I couldn't make out a single word they said.

Tired, achy, and sleepy after a day and a night of traveling, we finally arrived in Milano. A biting chill blew in the air. Uncle Frank met us at the station and we loaded ourselves and everything we owned into a taxi. He looked older than I remembered. So clean shaven, his cheeks shined when he turned around and ruffled my hair, smiling. Noisy cars, scooters, buses, bicycles, and trolleys were everywhere, and the buildings were so tall I craned my neck to look at them. There were no rivers, valleys, or high peaks. Most of all, the roads I had imagined to be lined with gold were paved with black tar and cobblestones that hurt the calluses under the soles of my feet. This was the world that had fed us, the world I'd dreamed of—the world that had robbed me of my father.

On the way to Nonna's home, we rode past row after row of apartment buildings. People hurried along sidewalks and in and out of shops. Cars crawled like ants in the streets. And just before we arrived, I saw in an open field dozens of children flying multicolored kites. Some hovered very high in the sad, hazy sky.

Uncle paid the driver and the taxi drove away. Still in my shorts, I shivered from the cold. Small shops lined the square, with a tobacconist's at the corner. At the curb, a stout man sat on a scooter with a wooden box with iced fish perched on the seat behind him. An accordion of apartment buildings bordered by green gardens and well-tended bushes faced us. On their balconies clothes hung on lines to dry.

Nonna's piercing voice hollered from one of the balconies when she saw us, and she welcomed us with open arms and exaggerated tears at the threshold. Located on the third floor of building number nine, street *Val di Bondo*, the apartment was spacious and clean. To me it looked like a palace. I felt strange with a slippery gray tile floor under my feet instead of earth.

Nonna had put on weight from what I remembered, but she carried it with style. She was about Mama's height, with streaks of gray in her coal-black hair and sparkling olive-green eyes that followed me everywhere.

I made the rounds of the house on my own while the rest of them stationed themselves in the living room with my family blabbering away. As I looked around the house, I wondered where she was going to settle us. A black and white wedding picture stared at me from the edge of a dresser. Mama had told me there had been some legal trouble between Nonna and my grandfather and the *Carabinieri* had given Nonna the right to get him out of the house. I wondered where he was staying.

The smell of food lured me into the kitchen. It was a narrow space with a refrigerator at the far end. An assortment of warped lids hung on the wall. A wood counter with white cupboards sat beside a four-burner stove on which two pots simmered. Nonna was stirring one. From under the lid of the other a thin trail of steam seeped out. She eyed me, smiled, and came over and wrapped me in her arms. He red apron smelled of garlic and oil.

The kitchen was small, but to me it offered all kinds of comforts. Back home, Mama had cooked over a steel tripod in the fireplace.

"*Va a salutari o Nonnu.*" Go and say hello to grandfather, Nonna said. She explained how to get there. I told Mama where I was going, and walked out.

On the way, I saw boys my age playing ball in the courtyard. I leaned against the building's frosty glass door and watched them. A skinny boy with curly black hair walked up to me and asked me something. I'd no clue what he was trying to say. His language was totally different from ours. I nodded, smiled, and said nothing. He waited for my answer. I nodded again. At last, he grimaced and walked away, yelling something to his friends.

I walked downstairs to the lower floor of the building. It was as dark as the cave where I used to fetch water. I stood a few moments letting my eyes adjust to the diminished light. There was a dank stench of rotting garbage, then I smelled a cigarette burning. I followed it, sniffing and groping along the wall, until I came to a small room. Someone coughed. A flash of fear passed through me. I peered inside. The shape of a man lying on a mattress in the tight room slowly emerged in the low light. What I could see of the head was bald, and the face was long, with a beak-shaped nose. "How you doing, *Nonnu?*" It had to be him.

"Who…who in hell are you?" his raspy voice called out. The head leaned forward, and the eyes squinted.

"It's me. Piero."

"Ooh." He groaned like a wounded animal and uncrossed one long leg. "When…when in hell did you get here?" he asked as if he had no idea we were coming. Probably Nonna hadn't even told him.

"Just now," I said, relieved to know it was really him. I could see him clearly now. He looked awful, with week-old gray whiskers.

"Ooh," he grunted again. He took a long puff of his cigarette. Blue smoke swirled in his face and rose toward the dim light bulb hanging from the ceiling. He coughed again, spat into a soiled handkerchief. What a depressing sight. There was nothing left for me to do but pay my respects to a man I felt a stranger to. This was the first time I had seen him in my life.

"Well, I'm going," I whispered, leaning against the cold cement door frame, waiting for some kind of reply. Nothing. I shuffled a couple steps back.

He let out another soft moan. Grandpa was great company.

I turned to walk away.

"*La signora* didn't waste any damn time getting you here." His words rang behind me with terrible bitterness. I wished somebody had slapped me instead. Nonna had married this man after her first husband died. And the warm feelings in my heart I longed to express toward this step-grandfather would probably never come out now. I had missed having a grandfather. And now as I stood there, I realized I'd never have one.

I slunk away in the dark, sad and unwelcome, headed toward the shaft of pale light coming in from outside, wondering what I might have done to be treated like this.

Outside it was raining. The sky was dark. The boys were gone and the courtyard was deserted. I leaned against the door and watched the rain splashing off the pavement, dripping from the rooftops, and gushing into the cement gutters with a swishing sound. What a strange new world this was, made of cement, asphalt, and beehives of apartments. I stood there a long time, numb, lost, watching the rain bounce off the ground. How was I going to get used to this? I wished I had wings to fly back to my village. Now it seemed a most beautiful place. But it was too late. There was no turning back, I sensed. But something I'd never seen before caught my eye. Everyone here wore shoes, children and adults alike. I looked down at my tennis shoes, and for a moment I felt like one of them.

Nonna had the long table set for lunch with plates of salami, prosciutto, green olives, *sarde*, anchovies, pickled eggplant, and slices of golden *ciabbatta*. I poured myself a glass of red wine and sat next to Uncle Frank. He was tall and lean with wavy black hair. He put his hand on my shoulder, leaned over and kissed me on my head. It felt so good, though I didn't know why.

After we had finished our lunch, dazed and sleepy from the wine, I wondered if grandfather had had anything to eat. I told Mama about it. She filled a plate with leftover pasta, scooped and spread two ladles of *ragù*, got a fork and a napkin, and handed them to me. "*Portalu o povaru diavulu.*" Take it to the poor devil, she said.

My first picture on Nonna's balcony. Behind me, her terracotta pots with her vegetables.

MEAT SAUCE

Serves 4-5

As a child growing up I never liked the sweet taste of carrots, onion, and celery that bled through the sauce Nonna made. This sauce is the result of my own experimenting over the years, and people at the restaurant relish it.

2 tablespoons of olive oil

2 tablespoons unsalted butter

1 ½ lbs ground chuck

2-3 oz dry white wine

16 oz canned Italian plum tomatoes, or canned diced tomatoes with no basil added. Use San Marzano if available

6 oz cream

6-8 oz marinara sauce

Salt to taste

If you prefer, you may split the above sauce with ½ lb of ground pork shoulder, veal, or both.

Puree tomatoes with their juice in a blender. Set aside.

In a wide saucepan, heat oil and butter over medium heat. Add the ground meat and stir with a wooden spoon to prevent meat from sticking. Cook until no raw flesh is visible, 7 to 10 minutes. Deglaze with wine and let it evaporate, 2-3 minutes. Add tomatoes and season lightly with salt. Bring sauce to a boil, cover partially, then reduce to a simmer. Let it cook slowly for about 1 ½ hours, stirring occasionally. During the last 10 minutes of cooking add the marinara sauce and cream. Stir and simmer. If sauce looks dry because too much liquid has evaporated, add some warm water and simmer a bit longer. This sauce can be made a day or two ahead. In that case, incorporate the cream into the sauce when you reheat it.

In a pot of boiling water cook a pound of pasta of your choice as described earlier. Drain and toss into sauce. Taste for salt and pepper. Let sauce coat the pasta. Add 2 oz of unsalted butter, and a generous handful of fresh grated Parmigiano. Serve at once with plenty of grated cheese.

SIX

The next morning Nonna's high-pitched voice rang in my ears. "*Svegliati, Bellu.*" Wake up. I felt her warm lips on my forehead, her soft hand on my face. Outside, it was overcast, a few gray clouds hovering low in the sky. The room was cold. It felt good to be under the blankets. I wished I could sleep in, but suddenly Nonna started undoing my covers, taking them out on the balcony, shaking them over the steel railings while she chuckled under her breath with delight. "You want to sleep in, eh? Go right ahead," she hollered.

The first major shock we encountered was the toilet. When Nonna sat on it to demonstrate its purpose. Silvio and I exchanged blank looks and nodded just to please her. For the next three or four days we trotted out to the open fields to answer the call of nature. Eventually, we become civilized like everyone else.

We had been there only a few days when Nonna and Mama decided to enroll me in school. It was located about five minutes' walk from the apartment, across from a church. When we got there, a nun greeted us. They were everywhere, dressed in white. The nun escorted Mama and Nonna into an office. I was told to wait outside by the door. I could see my distorted reflection in the shiny marble floor. Before long they came out with a frail, short, red-haired man. He mumbled something I didn't understand. For the first time it dawned on me how tough this new language was going to be, how I hadn't anticipated this difficulty. Nonna and the man rambled on about something for a while. Mama watched closely, trying to follow the conversation with her eyes. Then the nun took me by the hand and led me down a long hall. Mama and Nonna waved good-bye. The nun's hand felt sticky. She looked old and tired. A red pimple shined on her pointed nose.

It was a large all-boys classroom. A map of the country hung on the wall. Pictures of different species of birds covered the side wall. A clock hung above the teacher's desk. A fat boy next to me raised his eyes and smiled. Most of the other students turned around and stared at me. I felt so out of place I nearly panicked and ran, but I forced myself to stay.

Once the nun left, the teacher, tall and stocky with black curly hair, closed the door and asked me to introduce myself. I felt fear run up my spine like a flash of fire. I shook so hard my teeth chattered. How was I going to pull this off? I thrust one hand inside my pants pocket to feel for my little knife. When I was warm I used to put it on my forehead to cool myself off. I was hoping it would help now, but I didn't take it out.

Distraught, I stood up. All eyes descended on me. I started in proper Italian, but I soon ran out of words and began mumbling in my own dialect. Roars of laughter were all I could hear. I could feel the blood draining from my head, my face sizzling with shame, and a sense that I might black out at any moment. I wished I could disappear.

The laughter grew louder, and louder still. I couldn't stand it anymore. I ran to the door, yanked it open, and stormed out, the teacher calling my name. I ran down the steps, through the hall, out of the school gate, and into church, where I sat in an empty pew. My heart ached and my sobbing and moaning echoed in the big church.

I took out my handkerchief and dried my face. Eventually I stopped crying. I felt mad, sad, and sorry for myself. I rocked back and forth on the seat, banging my head against the pew in front of me, hoping to release some of my pain. I replayed the scene in my head over and over. "Why me?" was all I could think of. What a trade-off. At home I was poor, and everyone understood me. But here, in this place of great riches, I couldn't explain myself.

The church had tall multicolored glass windows, and black-draped booths along one wall. Statues of saints were lighted with rows of burning candles. An altar with Jesus nailed on the cross stood at the far back. A strong scent of incense hung in the air.

The handkerchief had become soaking wet, so I wiped my face on the sleeve of the old brown coat Nonna had given me to wear that morning.

A man's voice startled me. "*Perchè piangi?*" Why are you crying? A gray-haired priest emerged from behind me. I leapt up and ran down the long aisle. I couldn't wait to be out of his sight. He probably wanted some explaining. Suddenly, I slipped and landed flat on my face on the cold floor. How could this have happened? I was a good runner. Then it dawned on me. It was the fault of my black leather shoes. My jaw ached. I prayed to God I hadn't broken anything. Mama would kill me if I had.

"*Aspetta*." Wait, the priest hollered, his voice echoing inside the church. I scrambled to my feet, hitched up my trousers, and took off running again.

Outside, I took the church steps three at the time. I crossed the street and hid behind a *giornalaio*, a newspaper stand. I saw the priest in his long black robe, standing in the doorway. I had no intention of going back into the church. Or to school. Or home, or anywhere. If Mama knew about this, she would kill me. This was serious business. I could be expelled from school.

I wandered around behind the stand, looking at cowboys on horseback on the covers of magazines of the Far West. I wished I had wings to fly away and go to America. It seemed so far and so wild: endless.

I opened and closed my mouth a few times. My jaw was sore, but fine. I stood behind the kiosk, hiding from the cold, killing time, and staring at row after row of apartment buildings as far as I could see. The church bell tolled. The village, the mountains, and my secret spot in the poplar tree flashed into my head. After a while, I considered going back to school. After all, it wouldn't let out until three, and Nonna had said they served lunch at twelve thirty. I'd seen the kitchen, with its huge, steaming caldrons, when the nun took me upstairs. It had smelled good, too. But I wasn't sure I could face class again.

I was freezing behind the stand. I turned up the collar of the coat, stuck my hands inside its pockets, and stomped my feet on the ground to keep warm. I could see shoppers milling around at the fruit stand down the street. The bus depot was a few meters away, and the bus exhaust stung my eyes. The weather had turned gloomy, the sky dark. The skin on my face tingled and burned from the cold.

The little fellow from inside the kiosk came limping out and asked me what in hell I was doing there and why I wasn't in school—I think that's what he said. I looked at him and shrugged. I wanted to tell him to mind his own business, but I didn't know how to say it. I didn't like to be told what to do by a stranger. I sneered at him and left.

When I walked inside the school, I barely recognized the hall. Rows of tables joined in the middle of it. Plates, silverware, glasses, blue cloth napkins, and bottles of water lined the tables. The windows were fogged from moisture rising from the kitchen. I took a deep breath of the wonderful fragrances of the food, held them in my nose till my face turned red, then exhaled.

I climbed carefully up the waxed and shiny stairway to the second floor restroom to wash up, one hand sliding up the smooth wooden rail. The shoes Nonna had given me were a couple of sizes too big. They squeaked when I walked. No wonder I had nearly broken my neck on those steps.

I wondered where Nonna got the used shoes and coat. My hands hung inside the sleeves. But it kept me warm because, as the wrist label indicated, it was *pura lana*. Pure wool. That's all that really mattered.

Inside the restroom, I stared in awe at my reflection in the rows of mirrors. I was stunned. I'd never seen myself, except for an eye or a high cheek in the small cracked mirror back home. A thin boy with pointed shoulders stared back at me. Brown coat, red scarf, and gray trousers. A sad, sallow face, light brown hair, and bloodshot hazel eyes. I took off my coat and laid it on the heaters by the wall. I splashed water on my face. It was so cold I gasped for air.

Suddenly, I began sobbing and moaning again. With all the comforts this world offered, like indoor plumbing and electricity, I felt I didn't belong. I missed feeling my body sink into my cornhusk mattress, treating my baby goats to cubes of sugar even when they didn't deserve it, and staring at the snow-capped mountains that shimmered in the Calabrian sun.

I washed my hands and ran my fingers through my hair, watching myself closely as if I were looking at a stranger for the first time. I examined my face, my nose, noticing that I wasn't as ugly as I'd often imagined. I'd an ordinary face. A face I didn't really like. Then I smiled. I saw a decent smile.

There were so many bars of soap that I considered sticking a couple in my pocket and taking them home. My father went through one every day, I'd heard Nonna say, if she didn't hide it. But of course I could never take anything that wasn't mine. If I ever did, and Mama came to know, she would beat the living daylights out of me.

When classes let out, I walked into my classroom. The teacher looked at me with surprised eyes, as he slapped his hands clean of chalk. He came over and put his hand on my shoulder. "*Hai fame?*"

Yes, I was hungry. I could hear my stomach growling. I'd had only an espresso in the morning with a couple of Nonna's almond biscotti.

"*Andiamo,*" he said, and picked up his briefcase from the table. We walked out together, his hand on my shoulder. I was glad he was nice. I thought he might have gotten upset. I wondered if they were allowed to beat up students here. Well, at least I hadn't seen the wooden stick so far. That was a good sign.

Down the hall the girls sat at one end of the tables, the boys at the other. The teacher pointed me to a chair. Some of the students stared at me and giggled to one another. They were talking about me for sure. I felt anger rise in my chest, but then knew I was a stranger here, a "*Terrone.*" A no-good, inferior, uncivilized southerner. The owner of the bread shop had called me that and Nonna had explained it to me. The teacher waved them a warning.

Suddenly a loud whistle echoed through the hall. It was the little man from the office. The squeaking of his boots echoed as he strolled importantly down the hall. He tapped his thigh with a thin wooden stick in an even tempo. My heart dropped. Not even the buzzing of a fly could be heard.

All the students held out their hands palm up above the table. I put mine out too. Why else would they be showing their hands to him, other than to show if they were clean? Funny, with all our open hands we must have looked like beggars waiting for a *limosina*, a handout. The inspection completed, the nuns began prayers. I didn't know how to pray their way. I closed my eyes, hung my head, and listened to the chorus of monotone voices. Prayers went on for what seemed like hours. Then the nuns said "Amen," and I knew prayers were over.

I'd never sniffed so many delicious aromas at once in my life. I thought Nonna had been making up that stuff about the good food to make me go to school, but she was right. I'd have to stay in school at any cost now, for lunch alone.

"*Cosa vuoi tu?*" a lady cook asked when she got to the table with a cart loaded with food. What was she saying? I stared at her and shrugged. Irritated that I didn't give her an answer, she scooped something on to a plate from one of the trays, and handed it to me. "*Tieni*," she said. It was yellow rice, piping hot and so good I gulped it down and licked my plate clean. Some kids laughed at me, but I was too hungry to care. I stuck my tongue out at them. Then I realized there was more. I was given a plate of stew with peas in a light red sauce. Cheese came next, then dessert: pastries, slices of cakes, and fresh fruits. I was so full I thought I might burst. I had never even imagined that life could be so sweet and so filled with plenty.

From time to time, the teacher gave me a reassuring glance. I smiled back. It was cozy in the hall. A soothing warmth emanated from the kitchen. The smell of food hung in the air. I felt safe, for now. Outside, thunder roared and lines of fire flickered in the sky. Soon, rain blew in heavy gusts, battering against the windowpanes. Water gushed out from the rooftops and sluiced down the windows like snakes crawling in grass. I sat, full and happy. It was the best meal I'd ever eaten. I rubbed my stomach, leaned back in my chair, and smiled.

I was coming back the next day. How could anyone skip all this *grazia di Dio*?

Me, my brothers, an uncle and his daughter. In the background, the school where I ran out of class.

CHICKEN STOCK

Recipe for homemade chicken broth. (This is all part of the risotto)

Approximately 2 lbs beef bones

3 to 4 fresh parsley sprigs

2-3 carrots, peeled and chunked

1 medium white onion peeled and quartered

A whole chicken

Salt to taste

2 celery stalks, washed and chunked

Place all ingredients in a stockpot and fill it with cold water so that the ingredients are submerged about 3 inches. Cover with lid, ajar. Bring liquid to a slow boil on medium heat. Skim the foamy scum that comes to the surface with a skimmer or slotted spoon. Salt to taste. Reduce to low heat and let liquid simmer for an hour and a half.

Remove chicken. Let the broth simmer for an additional 10 minutes. If you plan to use the broth right away, strain it into another pot and use it. The rest can be strained and cooled off at room temperature and stowed in the refrigerator overnight, then skimmed of the fat that has formed on the surface in the morning. Freeze the rest and use as needed.

Naturally, there is an alternative to this if time doesn't permit: bouillon cubes, which lots of women use, as did my beloved grandmother. There are also other recent, less salty alternatives on the market, some of which are actually not too bad. But nothing compares with homemade broth.

RISOTTO ALLO ZAFFERANO E PORCINI

RISOTTO WITH SAFFRON AND PORCINI

Serves 4 to 5

8-9 cups of homemade broth	*1 oz reconstituted porcini*
1 tablespoon unsalted butter	*Saffron*
1 tablespoon olive oil	*1 oz cream*
1 medium white onion, finely diced	*A handful of fresh grated Parmigiano*
1 clove of garlic	*1 tablespoon of unsalted butter for finish*
2 cups of Arborio rice	
	Salt to taste
2 oz dry white wine	

In a colander, spray rinse the porcini under cold running water in a flash to expel most of the dirt. Add them to a small bowl containing 3-4 oz. of cold water. Let them steep in it overnight. Drain them into a sieve covered with cheesecloth to trap additional dirt. Remove reconstituted mushrooms, set water aside, and finely chop porcini.

Add 15 to 20 dry threads of saffron into a small bowl with 2 oz of lukewarm water and let sit for about an hour, then strain.

Place the chicken broth into a medium pan on low heat.

Place the porcini and its juice in a smaller pan on very low heat.

Heat butter and oil in a large skillet over medium heat. When the oil and butter heat up, add the onions, the garlic clove, stir with a wooden spoon and cook till the onions turn golden, 2 to 3 minutes. Remove garlic and discard. Add rice. Stir and cook until rice has been coated with the onion, butter, and oil, about a minute or so. Deglaze with wine. When the wine has evaporated and the skillet is starting to scream for liquid, rush to its rescue with a 6 oz ladle of warm broth, or enough to barely cover the rice. Incorporate the porcini and saffron liquid halfway through. Continue to cook and stir in this fashion, adding 6-oz. ladles of broth at a time, working it with the spoon, for about 18 minutes. At this point the rice should be tender but firm. As you cook, the rice will stick on the skillet's bottom. It's normal. Don't fear.

Add the cream, butter, Parmigiano. Taste and adjust for seasoning. Stir quickly and incorporate well for only a few seconds. Serve at once.

SEVEN

In less than a month Nonna got me a job. "*Figlio, devi aiutare anche tu.*" Son, you need to start helping, she said with a sense of urgency. I worked after school for the man who owned the fruit stand near the bus depot. At night I helped him roll the wooden cart to a warehouse. Short and stocky, he looked like a bulldog. But he swayed all over when he walked. He had polio. I helped him sort out the best fruits and stacked them on display in the front of the wagon, while he kept the bruised and overripe in the back to be sold first. I didn't like the idea of selling inferior produce to customers.

"What do you want me to do with it?" he asked the first time I told him it wasn't fair.

"That's how they sold them to me wholesale," he said. "You expect me to throw them away? What do you care anyway? Don't I pay you?" His brooding, crossed eyes lingered on me, defiant.

I didn't insist. I was afraid he might work himself into another frenzy, stagger and fall like he did a couple of times when furious costumers returned merchandise, complaining and demanding their money back. It was an ugly sight. I didn't want to go through that again. Spit foaming from his mouth, his body jerking uncontrollably on the ground like a pig being slaughtered, people rushing to the site, and me doing all the explaining. I didn't last long working for that man.

Then Nonna got me a job at a chicken shop across from the bus depot. There I had it made. I didn't have to worry about being out in the cold, snow, or rain, except when I delivered merchandise to customers. Sometimes I'd walk up six, seven, or nine flights of stairs for fear of getting stuck inside the elevator— my worst nightmare. My pay was *due mila lire*, less than two dollars, plus I was given a fat hen and plenty of eggs every weekend. This alone helped to put food on the table for a couple of days a week. This made Nonna happy, proud of her connections in the neighborhood—she boasted that with her abilities and intellect, she could have run the country much better than those crooked politicians who only thought to fill their own pockets—her words. Nonna could have led armies.

The pay I gave to Mama. But the tips from customers I saved. When I collected enough money, I'd buy myself a new pair of shoes from the dozens displayed in the show-windows. I could never figure why, with so many shoes in circulation in Milano, nearly all the people in my village went barefooted.

Once I finished elementary school, Mama enrolled me at the *medie*, a three-year middle-school course. I never questioned her decision, since the alternatives were much worse: technical courses to become an apprentice plumber, auto mechanic, electrician, or some other career I had no interest in at all. Now that my life had changed, I wondered what I might like to be when I grew up. But I'd no answer when other kids asked me. I'd brought my flute with me and I liked playing it. Sometimes the tunes came out pretty good. But one day the kids at school made fun of it, so I buried it inside an old black trunk grandfather had brought from America and never played it again.

Eventually I grew tired of pulling chicken feathers, skinning rabbits, delivering, and sweeping and mopping floors. I longed for something new.

My uncle Frank worked as a master butcher in the prestigious center of the city. The shop was located a block away from Piazza Cinque Giornate, where, in 1848, the Milanesi defeated Austrian troops after five days of intense fighting. Thus its name. My uncle got me a job there, but I'd no intention of becoming a butcher. I wanted something to appease my yearning; a way to better myself and discover what my life was all about.

I was out of the shop most of the time delivering on a bicycle that must have been about a hundred years old. It had wide handlebars, a bell, balding black tires, and steel brakes that squealed when I pressed them. Its steel frame was so old the gray paint had in parts faded, revealing the original metal below. A square, perforated metal box welded above the rear tire held my precious cargo. The bike was so heavy the insides of my thighs used to burn and ache when I pedaled it. It consumed liters of oil, which its loose chain splattered on my pants. I wore clothespins on my cuffs to spare my pants, but they didn't help much.

I delivered all over the city with that old clunker. We served some of the best restaurants in the area, like La Pesa, an upscale establishment, and also small family *trattorie* where quality and value were the main draw. The food served in many of these places was homey, like the *bollito misto*, *ossi buchi*, and *risotto*, typical of the region. Milano was unbelievable when it came to food. It was displayed just about everywhere you looked: in the open markets, restaurants, *rosticcerie*... And then there was the bread. It came in an endless variety of shapes and sizes: *ciabbatte*, *filoncino*, *michette*. Its aroma was suspended in the air everywhere and perpetually teased the senses.

To my stupefied eyes, Milano seemed like food heaven in comparison to the poverty of Calabria. These were two worlds so unlike one another, sometimes I felt as if I were in a foreign country. Food here was top priority for all citizens. Food shopping a daily ritual. And eating the national pastime. I must have wasted tons of hours over the years glued to shop windows observing the endless variety, colors, and patterns of food or pastries on display, while my salivary glands flooded my mouth with their juices.

When I returned to the shop—hungry—the boss complained. "*Dove diavolo sei finito?*" Where in hell have you been? His wife, a thin-hipped, middle-aged woman, would wag her finger at me and say, "There is a ton of deliveries waiting," and point to the big clock outside on the sidewalk.

I'd stare at the half-carcasses of beef that hung from steel hooks, dripping blood onto the sawdust-covered floor. I wasn't cut out for this line of work like my uncle was. I was constantly evaluating my choices, my reactions to my surroundings, the meaning of my life. I knew that this was no place for me. It would be only a matter of time before I moved on to something worthy of my efforts. I wanted to tell her to deliver the goods herself, to see what it was like riding their museum piece. But I kept my mouth shut out of respect for my uncle.

I could handle the heat, wind, cold, and usually even the dense gray fog that shut the city like a lid on a box. Sometimes the fog was so thick I couldn't see buildings a few feet in front of me. This unleashed unbearable attacks of claustrophobia and panic. But the rain and snow were pure torture. When it rained or snowed, Milano was a mess, and delivering under those conditions meant risking your life in the mad traffic.

One particular dreary winter day before Christmas, I was swamped with orders. This was the busiest day of the year. Everybody must have been in a happy mood for the phone rang non-stop. People were out shopping. The cafés swarmed with men, drinking in a haze of cigarette smoke, playing cards, or arguing soccer scores or politics—another national pastime. Grandmothers, mothers, and daughters slaved away in their kitchens at home to prepare the biggest feast of the year, while the men did nothing but show up when tables were set and ready, plopping themselves down like entitled kings.

The morning started out cold as ice, but that didn't bother me because I'd bundled up from head to toe like an Eskimo. Thank God I was able to make it through the morning shift. It was so cold my lips were dry and cracked, and my bones ached. We closed shop for lunch at twelve thirty. The boss and his wife, who lived nearby in a gated condominium complex, went home. Uncle and I walked across the street to one of the restaurants we served, *Il Moro*. My uncle liked to eat out. He had a very sophisticated palate, and was a good cook himself. Most butchers are.

Going out to eat with Uncle was always his treat. It was his way of showing me his affection and appreciation for my hard work. He knew the restaurant owner and the chef personally. As a delivery boy, I was insignificant, barely acknowledged when I delivered the goods. The chef came out and talked to Uncle every time, and would express his satisfaction, or rarely, his grievances, about the quality of the meat. And often the chef dove into long-winded explanations about the nuances of different sauces he used for various cuts of meat, or thanked Uncle for the porcini he brought him occasionally from Chiavenna. And while I tapped my feet under the table, ignored, Uncle learned new recipes.

We rarely ordered from the menu. We ate whatever the winds of the chef's temperament blew to our table. The waiter would come along soon after he left and bring us a plate of *bresaola*, cured beef sliced paper-thin, prosciutto, rectangular slabs of broiled polenta topped with melted gorgonzola cheese, and a pâté of olives spread over cubes of golden bread. Yes, it was a treat to go to lunch with Uncle.

That day, looking at the beautiful color combinations of the appetizers spread like a quilt over the table, something clicked in my head.

Why not become a chef?

It seemed creative, challenging, and even noble as a profession. I watched the round-bellied chef glide his way through the crowded dining room as if he were a little king, as if the world were his stage. I imagined his life being much better than that of a butcher's boy like me—breaking my back loading and unloading carcasses, walking in and out of the cold box, and risking my life in the traffic on that horrible bike every day.

It had begun to snow in chunks like wads of cotton. They plunged from the sky, blanketing the ground with white. The bicycle, leaning against the shop's wall, was getting covered. The red-tiled rooftops were becoming a white canvas.

Vitello ai porcini came as a second course after the tortellini *in brodo*. We finished with cheese, dessert, and coffee, then headed back to the butcher shop. As we crossed the street, the idea of becoming a chef buzzed between my ears like a trapped fly. Then a wave of icy grime splashed on my legs as a car dashed past. On the other side of the street, Uncle shook his head and roared with laughter.

But truly, deep inside, I'd no idea what I wanted to be. I was trying to understand what reason and purpose my life had in this world. I'd no clue where I fit in. I was constantly drawn toward the new and the unknown. Maybe there I'd find the missing pieces of my life, or maybe this desire was nothing more than a plan to escape my own unhappiness.

At the shop, I bundled up, cleared the snow from the bicycle, filled the basket, and headed out. I don't know how I managed to make it through the first round of deliveries in the traffic and snow. I headed back toward the shop, knowing there were still plenty to go. I decided to get off the particularly busy *Corso Ventidue Marzo* and take a shortcut back to the shop. I put out my left hand to let the drivers behind know I intended to turn. I stopped at the signal, where I removed the rubber hood of my raincoat, turned my head sideways, and waited for the tram to move on.

This was a long and wide boulevard flanked with apartments and office buildings and lined with shops on both sides which swarmed with shoppers at most hours of the day. To the east, it ran smack into Linate airport, and to the west, it ended a few blocks short of the Duomo.

I could see the massive war memorial commemorating the fallen soldiers of the Five Days battle squatting imposingly by the Piazza's rotunda, my line of vision now blurred with falling snow.

A trio of *Zampognari* stood on the corner. These were mountain people who came to town a few days before Christmas to earn a little extra money and to imbue and revive the Savior's spirit into the city dwellers with their holiday music. Dressed in their greenish traditional shepherd attire, inflated sheepskin bagpipes strung from their shoulders and red cheeks puffed from blowing into their flutes and pipes, they serenaded the passersby and the snow. People made their quick offerings and then melted away in the crowd. I watched, mesmerized, singing along under my breath to the beat of the sweet melody. *Tu scendi dalle stelle…O Re del cielo…* You descend from the stars, O King of the sky.

The trams were packed like sardines in a can, and by the time all the passengers got out, the signal had turned red again. The snow was falling thick now. It felt cold on my head. Fat white flakes melted on contact with the glistening cobblestones. The tram was taking too long to go. I pushed off the ground with my left foot and started the turn. When I got on the tracks the front tire slipped and I landed face down in the middle of the tracks. The bicycle slid away across the slippery cobblestones. At the same time I heard the tram take off. I knew this was it for me. My short, inconsequential life flashed before me in an instant. I could hear the slippery screeching of the brakes, steel rubbing against steel. The driver must have seen what had happened. In seconds, I was covered by darkness as the tram slid above my head. Terror struck me so deeply I felt like the air I was gasping had turned to rocks. I pressed my body lower into the ground, wishing there was a way to dig a hole and save my life. I wanted to scream for help. I didn't want to die like this. I reached out in my head and implored God, if there was one, to rescue me. The sharp, hissing, screeching sound of the brakes sounded distant, muffled by the thudding of my heart in my ears.

Then I heard and saw something I would never forget. The steel wheels on both sides of me screeched to a halt.

"*Non ti muovere*," the driver said, peering under the tram on his hands and knees, "until I back it up."

Once the tram reversed, I was up in a flash. A few more centimeters and the cable box under the tram would have crushed my skull. I looked up at the sky and under my breath thanked my lucky star.

A crowd had gathered. A low murmur spread among the spectators. Dazed, I heard faint voices asking if I was all right, if they should call an ambulance. I forced a feeble smile, shook my head, and said I was fine. The shaking and a choking sensation came on with a vengeance now. I felt like I was about to pass out. An internal trembling seized my body. I summoned all my mental strength to fight the battle raging inside me. Strangers picked up the bicycle, brought it over to me, and stood staring with sympathetic eyes.

Naturally, that old clunker of a bicycle was fine.

It would outlast the earth.

I crossed the street and walked down the sidewalk in a trance, my legs wobbly, past buildings and shops, glancing toward the tracks running in the middle of the road—the tracks where I could have been lying dead.

When I got to a familiar building, I lifted the bike on my shoulder, entered, walked down the cement steps, and laid the bike against a dark wall. I stood for a moment remembering all the aching muscles and sweat it had made me endure. I patted the black saddle. Then I climbed up the stairs and out onto the sidewalk again. I drew another deep breath. I was feeling better—the panic attack was subsiding. I held out my hand, caught some falling snow, and moistened my cracked lips with it.

The next day would be Christmas.

I looked up at the shower of millions of snowflakes tumbling down from the sky and was grateful I had just been given a new chance at life.

I entered a café next door and called the boss on the phone. I told him to come and pick me up in his new Townsend, for somebody had stolen the bike. He paused for a long while at the other end of the line, and then asked, "Have they stolen the deliveries?"

VITELLO AI PORCINI

VEAL WITH PORCINI

Serves 4

2 tablespoons olive oil

2 tablespoons butter

1 lb veal round, sliced about ¼ inch thick, equaling a total of 12 to 16 slices

12 oz crimini or shitake mushrooms, or both, wiped with a damp cloth, then sliced

3 oz of chopped scallions

3 garlic cloves, minced

2 oz dry white wine

1 oz dry porcini mushrooms, with 1 oz of its water

Salt and pepper to taste

Minced flat leaves of Italian parsley

Follow previous method for preparing porcini.

Slice and pound the veal into little medallions of about 1 oz each. If you know a good butcher ask him to prepare it for you. It will save you time and work.

Place a very large skillet on medium heat. Dust each cutlet lightly with all-purpose flour. Shake off excess flour, and place slices into hot oil. Cook for about 5 seconds on each side, remove and transfer onto a warm platter.

Add the sliced mushrooms to the skillet, and cook 4-5 minutes. Mushrooms absorb oil like sponges. If they look dry add a bit more oil, but not too much. Add scallions and cook for about a minute. Add the veal and its juices, the garlic, and stir. Deglaze with wine. Add porcini and its water. Season with salt and pepper to taste. Add a generous dash of butter, parsley. Serve. If you'd like, leave a little sauce behind, and flavor pasta of your choice with it.

EIGHT

Domenica was the only day we lunched together at Nonna's long dining room table. Everyone was off work. The shops were closed, except cafés and cinemas. Mama and Nonna were up early in the kitchen chopping onions, parsley, and garlic and stuffing veal cheeks or other concoctions while the invariable *ragù* simmered away. In winter the dining room windows were fogged up with moisture rising from boiling pots of *bollito misto* or minestrone soup on the stove. Occasionally Uncle Frank showed them how to cook certain cuts of meat like veal cutlets, calf's liver, sweetbreads, calf's brains, pig's feet, or braised beef shoulder which had been marinating in red wine all night.

In the late afternoon, after everyone had played a few rounds of *briscola*, a card game, we drank *espresso macchiato* with *sambuca*. After some of us had dozed off into a satisfying nap, Uncle Frank would take me to the Cinema Colosseo on his Vespa. We saw *The Magnificent Seven* at least six times, and *Rio Bravo* with John Wayne probably a dozen. But Uncle didn't much care for *Dr. Zhivago*. He slept and snored like a sputtering lawn mower through most of it. I marveled at the imaginations of the people who wrote these stories, and thought that being a writer might make an interesting life.

Invariably we wound up the day at the café next to the butcher shop, where Uncle played poker for money with a bunch of pimps for hours on end. I watched through the window as people scurried down the busy sidewalk in the freezing cold with coats clutched to their chests and scarves flapping. And as the steel-gray sky melted away into night, another day, and another week, slipped away. When he won, Uncle would throw me a smile and a wink and offer for me to get whatever I wanted from the bar, and plenty of *Nazionali* cigarettes. But when luck deserted him, his face darkened, his eyes narrowed, and rarely, when he caught someone cheating, a fistfight would break out.

Occasionally I thought about the mountains, the village, and the goats we'd left behind. The old mother goat had refused to eat after we left. Aunt Rosa said in her letter that all the old thing did was bleat all day long, staring south toward our old home. Aunt Rosa put the animal out of her misery a month later. I sobbed the night Mama gave me the news. But as time passed it all became hazy, like a dream.

Mama struggled to adjust to city life. She detested being cooped up inside an apartment, and confided to me that she missed the open spaces, picking and curing olives, tending her garden, making cheese, and drying tomatoes and figs in the warm Calabrian sun. Before long, my father rented a small parcel of land outside the city limits. We had a garden once again. Mama's eyes sparkled at the notion that she would be working her own small plot of land. I knew my parents were trading their lives to provide us with a better future. For the first few years I saw Milano as a jungle of asphalt and cement. The bitter cold winters didn't help matters. But by slowly expanding my circle of friends, going to school, and working, I got used to the city.

I'd no other choice.

Father got a job in construction as a *manovale*, a laborer. Mama took my brothers to kindergarten each morning and then retreated back to the apartment to help Nonna with house chores: mopping and waxing the floor, hand-washing clothes and hanging them to dry on the balcony, beating mattresses out of windows, and peeling and snapping heaps of string beans for dinner's *contorno*.

One of the major adjustments of life in Milano, besides the language, was sharing so little space with so many family members. There was my married aunt, her husband and their two female toddlers, another aunt, and of course Uncle Frank and Nonna. My most painful experience was waiting in line to share the apartment's single bathroom with them each morning. Silvio, in extreme emergencies, still hopped down the stairs and out into the fields.

Grandpa had settled in downstairs, and it seemed to me he'd be there indefinitely now that we had taken over his room. In the morning he worked for a firm as an assistant clerk for a few hours, then spent the rest of the day at the café down the street playing cards to supplement his meager war pension. And when he wasn't doing that, he chased beautiful women. He was a notorious womanizer, and I think this was the real reason Nonna threw him out of the house.

Every night when Grandpa came upstairs for supper, he made his discontent known to us in a hundred little ways. His defiant, puffy eyes gazed at each of us in turn, as though we were responsible for his miserable condition. And yet after dinner he often serenaded Nonna as if hoping to win her back. But she didn't seem to pay any mind to the passionate notes that surged from Grandpa's violin or guitar. His eyes and his music followed Nonna in and out of the kitchen, his warm voice bellowing old Argentinean tangos. But the melodies seemed destined to flow out of the balcony, into the quiet evening air and over the treetops, hover over the tobacco shop, and fade into the warm summer night. If Nonna heard them, she gave no hint. None. "Ah, you people have no appreciation for music," Grandpa would grumble, exasperated, standing and putting away his instrument when Nonna denied him even a tender glance. *La musica non muore mai.*

A couple of years passed. I couldn't stand the lady boss or the boring work at the butcher shop anymore. I was tired of staring corruption in the face every time the health inspector came in. Uncle and the boss loaded him like a donkey with prime cuts of beef and veal—cuts we could never afford. It wasn't my nature to tolerate these humiliating and unjust practices. This, more than the grueling work, fueled my desire to leave. There had to be a place where a young man could retain his dignity, his self-respect.

Could America be that place?

I told Uncle I was quitting. He tried convincing me to stay, but I didn't give in. Finally, he reluctantly agreed that butchering wasn't my trade. He also knew that once I fastened onto an idea, I wouldn't let go.

I landed a job as a *fattorino*, a clerk's assistant. My parents idolized blue-collar work as the ultimate accomplishment in life, and I liked office work because it was light and clean. But shuffling papers all day was boring. The only bright side to this job was this flirtatious brunette full of curves who worked in the office. I confess that's why I'd taken the job. She never gave me the time of day, however. I stayed on for some time, but I got tired of giving her the eye in vain. When I realized no miracle would ever take place, I left. At seventeen, it was my first bittersweet taste of love.

Mama didn't like my moving from job to job. "What's the matter with you? Why can't you stick with one job instead of moving around like a butterfly? That's the only way you'll get ahead in life." Then she'd quote her favorite proverb—she'd one for almost all occasions—"The rock that doesn't develop mildew, every flood will wash it away." I was supposed to be a mildewed rock. Sure, like I believed in *Babbo Natale*, Santa Claus. As if I couldn't see the fresh trickle of blood on father's arm from the sore on his shoulder he got from carrying buckets of cement for new apartment projects. Or the sad mosaic of dried plaster on his neck and face and in his hair when he sat down on an upturned bucket to eat the lunch I brought him. The merciless sun of summer had burnt his skin and cracked his lips. Cement dust glazed his eyes. He earned barely enough money in a month to pay our portion of the rent, utilities, and food.

Was this what Mama wanted for me? To stay with such dead-end jobs? I had their blood coursing through my veins, but my parents had no clue.

I was of another stamp.

With hopes of bettering my lot in life, I got a job in a restaurant as prep, dishwasher, and everything else under the sun. The idea of becoming a cook still simmered in my head. After all, it seemed a profession that required a certain sensitivity. And that was something I had plenty of—too much at times.

Although the chef looked like a scarecrow from the cornfields outside Milano, it was a pleasure to watch him as he moved about the stove with grace, speed, and coordination, like a *ballerino* on stage. His hands gripping the skillet's handle, he pitched it forward and the food rose up in a heap, flew off the skillet's rim, and broke in midair like a wave. To watch him do this was the highlight of my day—whenever he dashed to the dining room to help his disconsolate wife, I'd lunge furtively and try to flip it myself, often spilling part of it on the floor.

But soon the restaurant seemed like another dead end job, and working alongside this purple-faced drunk was beginning to get to me. Every day he was in and out of the café next door getting bombed on *prosecco*. I often wondered how in the world he could manage to cook as well as he did in such a state. But he never missed a beat. Chopping carrots, onions, celery, and mincing parsley, his hands moved with mind-boggling precision and speed. Some days he was unbearable to be around. He threw pots, pans, knives, and lids, and yelled at me and his other helper to work faster. There were many times I wanted to tell him off and walk out. But I needed the money, so I gritted my teeth and kept my mouth shut.

Free lunch was the only benefit of working there, as the pay was well below standard. But the drunken tyrant's food was so flavorful it remained in my memory, along with a few tricks of the trade I picked up from watching him. *Vitello tonnato*, veal with a tuna and caper sauce, was my preferred dish. It's a typical Milanese summer dish, served cold and drenched with a velvety sauce. And for the short time I worked there—less than two months—that's mostly what I ate.

One day, in the throes of lunch, upon the scarecrow's loud command I grabbed a broiling skillet from the oven only to feel my flesh stick to the searing handle. *Figlio di puttana.* Later, in self-defense, he claimed he'd told me to use a towel. For all I know he could have been lying. But how could I have been so dumb? That taught me a lesson: always use a towel.

I couldn't stand him anymore, and whatever desire had been in me to become a cook was gone. One day my patience ran out. I lost my temper. I blew up and did what I had contemplated for so long: I told him off. I saw the blood drain from his cheeks. I demanded to be paid on the spot. And walked out.

My next job was as a clerk's helper with an upholstery company. It was another of those fancy occupational positions where I was promised the world and later they made me do everything: deliver on yet another—newer—bicycle, mop floors, sweep outside the building with a push-broom, and get espresso from the corner café for the boss and the mousy mistress he called his secretary.

Sunday lunch at Nonna's. We took turns eating. We couldn't all fit. Nonna, uncle Frank, me and my brothers.

VITELLO TONNATO

VEAL WITH TUNA SAUCE

Serves 4-6

2 lb boneless veal loin, or the rump. Eye of round is best for this dish.	*3 tablespoons capers, rinsed and drained*
	3 anchovy filets
1 carrot, 1 celery stalk, 1 medium white onion, chopped coarsely	*¼ cup mayonnaise*
5 sprigs of flat-leaved Italian parsley	*½ cup olive oil (approximately)*
	Juice of 1 lemon
3 ½ oz imported canned tuna, drained	*Black pepper to taste*

Place veal, carrot, celery, parsley, and onion in a large saucepan and cover with cold water. Bring to a boil, reduce to a simmer and cook for 1½ hours. Let veal cool in the same water, extract and dry. Wrap with plastic and place in refrigerator for 4-5 hours.

In a food processor or blender, puree tuna, capers, and anchovies. Add mayonnaise, lemon juice and oil, and stir to a fine consistency. Add pepper, and salt if needed. Slice cold veal into thin slices, approximately ¼ inch thick. Arrange on a flat platter, slightly overlapping, and spoon sauce over it. Veal should be drenched with sauce. Cover well with plastic and place in refrigerator overnight. Remove and garnish with capers and lemon slices. Serve.

NINE

One day a relative from California showed up on Nonna's steps. It was Mama's first cousin, Aunt Mary's older boy, with his wife. I was the first to face them when the bell rang and I opened the door.

"Who in hell is it now?" Nonna's piercing voice called out from the dining room. I stood in awe in front of them, one hand on the door handle. The man was a towering figure, with a benevolent smile and chestnut hair parted to the side. The woman was much shorter, with freckles scattered over a face as pretty and round as a doll's.

Nonna approached with scrutinizing eyes, holding her dull butcher knife downward by her side. "*Chi sono?*" Who are they? she demanded, her eyes in transit between them and me. Naturally, she had to check everything that crawled under the sun.

"*E che ne so?*" And what do I know? I said, shrugging.

She got hold of my elbow and pulled me gently to the side, her curious eyes studying the visitors like a cat studies a mouse.

The man spoke dialect well, but with some foreign accent, and soon explained who they were. His eyes traveled between the knife and Nonna as he spoke. The man's wife looked at him with a gleam of admiration in her eyes. Nonna stood motionless, but all ears. When the man finished his introduction, she considered his words, brought her hand to her chin, and tried to make sense out of it all. When the answer came to her, she smiled as if she had known them all along, and motioned them inside. Then she turned to me. "*Sbrigati,* son. Clear the table and get them something to drink."

I was so fascinated to find out who these relatives were, I stood there in a daze, my head spinning and traveling across the Atlantic, thinking that my star was conspiring to fulfill my desire to go to America.

"*Che aspetti?*" What are you waiting for? Nonna whispered. "Don't stand there like Wednesday in the middle of the week." I had been helping her cut a head of lamb in half to make soup with, and the dining room table was a mess. Blood and shards of bone were everywhere. A hammer we had tried to use—unsuccessfully—to pound the knife into the skull sat in the middle of it all. It could have been the scene of a murder. I bolted through the dining room and swept up the tablecloth with everything in it. I ditched it in the kitchen, then spread a clean tablecloth and poured two glasses of Orangina while Nonna kept the visitors busy with her loud ritual talk.

Once they were accommodated and the formal preliminaries were over, Nonna plied them with questions cleverly crafted to reveal her chief concern: how much money they had. The man started unraveling the whole ball of yarn about his family, the property he owned, and the factory he had just sold. Soon a subtle, mischievous smile appeared on Nonna's face and she started wailing and whining about how difficult life was for all of us. Probably hoping this rich Americano would shell out a few hundred dollars so that she could stash it under her mattress, where she kept her money wrapped inside a brown oil-stained apron. She moved in and out of the kitchen, blabbering the whole time.

The kitchen was the engine that ran her life—the center of her universe. It was her confession booth, where her blessings, counsels, and admonitions were dispensed over the simmering pots and pans. It was the bridge that supported us, and the glue that kept us together. Everything in our lives seemed connected with the yellowish, oily, worn-out door panel her fingers grabbed dozens of times a day. Nonna's presence seemed to be the source of life for each and every one of us. She was the sun that never set.

After a while she got on the phone and told Uncle we had important company and to bring home plenty of meat for dinner.

Soon Mama came home. She was so excited to meet her first cousin that she was pouring out tears of joy in no time. She had been corresponding with Aunt Mary over the years, but this was a total surprise. It wasn't every day you met a relative all the way from America.

Nonna was making a racket in the kitchen, clanging pots and pans as she dug them out from the cupboards. Sometimes during the summer with the kitchen window open, I could hear her from the street as she cursed and yelled at the lack of space and her *mala sorte*. Oftentimes, I crouched, laughing. Nonna had had a hard life. That was the main reason she had accepted Grandfather's offer to move the family to Milano. And in many ways it had turned out to be a good move. Although Nonna still complained about the heavy air, the bitter winters, and the cloudy sky, she had embraced the city like most Calabrians, because Milano offered a future to everyone.

When I went in to see if she needed a hand she shook her head, pursed her lips, waved me away like I was the devil. But a minute later I could forget about getting away. Nonna always had chores for me: Wash and dry dishes with a towel. Peel and chop onions, carrots, garlic, celery, the parsley she grew in terracotta pots on the balcony. These were the basic ingredients of her cooking. And there was nothing in the world better than a plate of *pasta al pomodoro*, according to her. I tried to teach her to make risotto and polenta a few times, which I had learned by stealing glances at the scarecrow. But she pushed me aside and scowled. "That's food for the *polentoni Milanesi*," she grumbled, "not us."

Father, Grandpa and my uncle came home after a while. Another round of introductions took place, and we all stood up around the table and toasted. *Salute.* Shortly afterward, Uncle excused himself and disappeared into the kitchen, with Nonna at his heels.

Uncle's favorite way to whip up a quick meal when we had unexpected company was to slice thin steaks and grill them on the open flame. In half an hour he had a meal ready, including a side of fried peppers and onions.

When dinner was over, Mama took Al into our room. I followed them. Al's blue eyes fell on the dismal little room, the tiny makeshift kitchen in the corner, and out of the window. Mama offered him a chair at the kitchen table, and fired away. She told him we still had no idea if or when the government would give us an apartment and, without further ceremony, asked him if he could help us go to America. He scratched his bushy eyebrows and considered. Then he told her he would do anything possible to help. Fresh tears of joy welled up in her eyes, and a little smile emerged and settled on the contours of her lips. Visions of cowboys on horseback in the endless prairie formed in my head. That faraway land I had dreamed of now seemed to be within reach.

Later in the evening Mama offered her bed to Al and his wife, according to our own custom. We were going to sleep in the living room, but Al said they had a reservation at a hotel and all he needed were directions to get back to it. I offered to be their guide, and escorted them with Uncle's old blue Vespa.

I had never seen a Hilton on the inside. It was expensive looking, with uniformed personnel at the entrance bowing with ceremonial dignity at everyone entering the engraved glass doors. Al invited me up to their room. What luxury and excess! I felt like a *pesce* out of water. Then he gave me one of his business cards and told me to get ready—that before long he would have me in the States.

As I drove home through the glaring night streets, silent explosions of joy were erupting inside my head. I gripped tight onto the handlebars of the scooter, for it felt like I was floating from the excitement. After I crossed the tracks, near the field of kites, I could smell the scent of flowers floating in the night air from a nursery along the road.

The whistle of a train shattered the night. Then it rattled by and sped down the tracks, leaving a hollow silence behind.

BISTECCA DELLO ZIO ALLA GRIGLIA
UNCLE'S GRILLED THIN STEAKS

Serves 2

If you don't own a small portable grill, get yourself one. It's worth the small investment, and you won't be disappointed. Grills are very versatile for cooking vegetables, fish, chicken breasts, and thin steaks, all in the blink of an eye. Well… almost.

Buy a beef rib-eye cut of about a pound or two. You can freeze what's left over.

A pinch of dry oregano

1 tablespoon of extra virgin olive oil

Salt and pepper to taste

Cut 5 to 6 steaks lengthwise in ½ inch thick slices, and set aside.

Place grill on stove's burner at medium heat and let it get hot, about 1- 2 minutes.

Place meat on hot grill, cook for about a minute or so on each side. Transfer meat into a medium-sized bowl. When finished, sprinkle with oregano, oil, adjust for salt and pepper, mix. Serve at once with a side of mixed green salad.

TEN

Soon, Al's letter came with the plane ticket. This was it. I was out of my wits from the excitement. Going to America at twenty. What a lucky man!

Mama saw no reason for me to leave now that we had our own home. She tried convincing me to stay. "How are we going to manage without you, *figlio mio?*"

"You will manage," I said, watching her hang clothes on the lines out on the balcony of our eighth-floor apartment. A jungle of apartment buildings sprawled beyond it under a pale midday sky.

"Just don't understand why you have to leave now that we have our own place. And besides, Angela told me she is sad to see you go. Doesn't she mean anything to you?"

No, she didn't. She was a chubby brunette who lived on the floor below. She'd two large pimples on her forehead, and wore thick spectacles. Every time we rode the lift together, I stared at the floor to avoid her intense gaze, thinking what would happen if the lift got stuck between landings. Would she come at me, pressing her lips against mine to soothe my panic attack? I wouldn't have put it past her.

"Why can't you stay home and be happy like everyone else? You think that by moving to another country you can solve your life's problems? That's not the way it is, my dear. You can't run from yourself."

Mama always had a way of rationalizing things to the point that they even made sense to me. She would have made an excellent courtroom attorney. It was true that life had improved since we'd moved into our apartment. But Mama couldn't see that my meaningless job was choking me, that I didn't stand a chance of fighting this monster of a bureaucratic system that was so riddled with injustices and favoritism. I could never have achieved much. I was a peasant's son first, a *Contadino* who had worked for the rich Dons in the area, hoeing vineyards, harvesting grain, picking grapes—sometimes for no money, but only a plate of pasta with stale bread, and plenty of wine—sometimes diluted with water to stretch it, to make the rich fatter, to dull the workmen's senses. I was an *Operaio*, an unskilled laborer's son in Milano. My father worked on roads, apartment projects, and later, at a car manufacturer. It would be difficult for me, if not impossible, to break these ranks without the proper recommendations and connections. Connections I detested. A man should have the right to become what he wants based solely on his abilities and hard work. No system. No one should obstruct a man's desire to better his life, to get ahead, to see his dreams came true. And besides, what had my father accomplished with all his hard labor, his sweat, the deep gashes in his palms produced by a shovel's handle? He'd been getting up at four in the morning, rain or shine, as far back as I could remember. Father didn't know that a lifetime of shoveling and digging would accomplish nothing. What did he have to show for it? Nothing really. Living from paycheck to paycheck, working like a mule, rolling his own cigarettes to economize, while Mama scrambled to save a few Lire every day.

I compared my country to a parent that can't provide for his own children, clothe them, take care of them. I blamed it for leaving family, friends, my land. But I was determined to pull my own strings in life, follow my intuition. "Because someday I don't want to have regrets," I snapped. "That's why, Ma."

Why couldn't I be like everyone else? After all, one life was probably as good as another. "*Ricordati che il mare e' tutto salato.*" Remember that all of the sea is salty. Another of her proverbs. I couldn't stand them.

Soon I'd be leaving my family and friends for a place I'd only dreamed of. And who knew what awaited me across the Atlantic? What future lurked in store for me? And what kind of life would I renounce by leaving? That I'd never know.

My heart thumped with anticipation. The world seemed mine.

I gave notice at work, parted with friends and relatives.

Still, I dreaded my departure, sensing Mama might start crying and screaming at me not to leave. It would tear my heart to see her like that. Luckily, Nonna was strong. She'd be there for Mama to lean on. She was a good buffer for me. I had to admit I was lucky to have this family even if they were imperfect.

Grandfather, who had become softer with time, tried to discourage me from leaving a good-paying job, family, and friends. To go to a strange continent with relatives I didn't know, and turn my back on a city that offered opportunities for everyone, must have seemed crazy to him. He shook his head in disapproval and muttered that going fishing and hunting now wouldn't be the same without me. His comment surprised and flattered me.

That night before I left, I saw Mama light a candle and place it on the dresser in front of the picture of Saint Anthony. She knelt on the floor, doubled over her bed with her hands together. I tiptoed closer, and caught snippets of her supplications: *Watch over him, Archangel Michael. Father, give me the strength to let him go. May he find what he is looking for...*

I retreated to my room, stared at a poster of New York's Twin Towers at night. Then I shut off the light and looked out my window enveloped in the darkness and aware of the rise and fall of my chest with each breath. I watched people come and go from a café below. Funnels of headlights streamed down the dark highway beyond the distant soccer field where I'd played countless times.

I closed the window and went to bed.

In the morning the house smelled of fresh-brewed coffee. Mama poured me an espresso from the *caffettiera*, sweetened it with two cubes of sugar, and handed it to me. I glanced at her as I brought the cup to my lips. Her eyes were red and puffed up from crying and lack of sleep. My heart ached to know that she would miss me. For as much as I tried to display a tough exterior, deep inside I needed her. She was my anchor, my point of reference. I wasn't afraid to embark on a new journey. In fact, that was the thrill, the beauty of it all, not to know what lay ahead, what awaited me. For I knew I'd the strength to survive anywhere. Those years in Calabria had made me resilient in spirit like an olive branch.

I took a quick tour of the apartment one last time, wondering where I'd be sleeping that night. I forced back the tears that had been threatening to spill all morning.

The family accompanied me to the Malpensa airport. It was a cold, overcast April day. I could hardly believe I was about to go away for who knew how long. Leave family and friends for a world so distant and unknown. The city seemed brighter that morning, as though the buildings along Amoretti Street where we lived were smiling as we drove past them. The excitement in my heart seemed to color the world. But Mama was sad, and so were the nearly a dozen relatives who drove along in separate cars to see me off. I'd never imagined I meant that much to any of them. I'd miss my uncle above all. He'd become like an older brother. A bond had developed between us like I'd never known before, and as a result, I loved him out of all proportion.

I was the first of my generation to break away like this. It wasn't as popular to go to America in the seventies as it had been when Al's parents left Calabria in the twenties. And it was certainly not as difficult as then either. This was only my second major journey since I'd first left Calabria at ten. I wondered what my third journey would be, or if there'd be a third.

For the future lay inscrutable like darkness.

At the airport, I checked my suitcase at the TWA counter. I remembered my father standing with his suitcase by the school grounds. What was the summation of my life now? Desire seemed the only element propelling me. The same unrequited desire that had plagued me in Calabria, when as a boy I used to contemplate scaling the mountain range someday.

That same desire was alive in me now. It had never left me.

We milled around the boarding gate waiting for departure. Mama clung to my arm like a snail to a windowpane. Soldiers with machine guns slung over their shoulders and German shepherds on leashes strolled the premises. Although I was sad about leaving my family, the excitement to see America was overwhelming. Mama shook me from my daze and reminded me to call her when I got to America, to wear my wool undershirt at all times, and to be careful of strangers. I nodded, but didn't make eye contact with her for fear I might break down before she did. An invisible pair of hands seemed to constrict around my throat. I took a deep breath, praying I wouldn't have a panic attack now.

As I looked at the circle of relatives surrounding me, I felt their love, their bond. I could also see in their eyes a resignation to a life that bore down on them with its weight, its demands, obliterating any ambition they might have had, leaving them helpless, disillusioned. There was also something else in their expressions. They were pinning all their hopes of success on me, as if I was the pathfinder, the savior, when in reality, I doubted how my own life would turn out in the New World.

Then I only remember the announcement of a loudspeaker echoing through the small airport. Suddenly a blur of faces were kissing me on the cheeks, hands clapping my shoulders and tugging at my lapels, and eyes flowing with tears. I fought my way out of the circle of relatives and pushed through the gate. I could hear Mama crying and Nonna consoling her. Hers were tears of anguish that she might never see or hear from me again. For in Calabrian folklore, a voyage is regarded as a possibility of no return, death. I gritted my teeth, toughened my heart, and walked down the aisle without turning around.

Before long, the plane was ready for takeoff. This being my first time flying, I was thrilled and a bit scared, wondering how such a metal monster could lift off the ground. But in minutes it climbed the sky, and the Padana Valley below shrank into a distant dot. I peered through the window as the world that had shaped me, had meant everything, receded like a fragment of time.

Strapped into my seat, I stared at the endless valleys of thick white clouds. I remembered the days as a goatherd when with my outstretched hand I brushed the sky and these very clouds. Where had the little shepherd boy gone? I wondered again what America might have in store for me. And what was I searching for? Maybe someday I'd find the answer.

I leaned my head against the window, took in a portion of the uncertain sky, closed my eyes, and let my mind wander.

It is one of those limpid days when I can see for kilometers. I lie on my back in the dry grass under the poplar tree looking up into the cloudless blue sky. I can hear my goats nibbling on low branches. They are docile animals, but I need to be vigilant, for in an instant they can sneak into a vineyard nearby and wreak havoc. And then Mama will kill me for sure. In the sky a plane is passing, a trail of vapor streaking behind it like the wake of a ship. I wonder how it can fly, where it is headed, and what it might look like inside. I extend my hand and feel as if I can touch it. Then I hear Mama's piercing voice echoing from the house below. I wonder what chore she has lined up for me next.

The image of Mama's teary eyes and wailing at the airport was still echoing in my head. If there was something I detested more than anything, it was to see her cry. I should have been used to it after so many years, but I wasn't, would never be. For my heart disintegrated one little piece at a time every time she wept. And wept.

"Welcome…New York," an English voice announced through the speakers as we were about to land. I wasn't able to understand the rest of the announcement, as I opened my eyes from sleep, startled. Months of English night classes at the Commercial Institute in Via Fabio Filzi were proving almost useless now. All those evenings when I struggled to keep my eyes open as I listened to strange verb conjugations, senseless vocabulary, and a pronunciation that wracked my brain, seemed wasted now.

I could hardly believe I was in America. Hands clapped as the wheels touched ground. Passengers cheered. My heart fluttered. A few tears of joy formed in my eyes. I was overwhelmed, and my restless eyes didn't know which way to peer. I looked over the plane's wing. There was hardly anything to see, except airport employees loading luggage onto conveyer belts. But a new continent lay at my feet. Truly this was the New World. My childish instinct wondered if these streets might also be paved with gold. But I was no child to believe in such dreams any longer.

We were guided down a brightly-lit tunnel into a hall where customs officers directed the flow of human traffic. I was shocked to notice a sea of ethnicities gathered under one roof. It was the first time I'd been in such close proximity to so many races. So many colors, features. So many cultures, really. I felt strange and out of place. So this was America, the allure of the world. This was the place I'd dreamed of for so long, every time I slid my fingers over those magic numbers indented on the wall in the darkness. The place so many longed for.

I stood there in the crowd, rooted like a post, my eyes roving around the giant pavilion, dazzled. Suddenly I imagined the millions that had come before me, through that not too distant harbor, on boat's decks, stretching their arms toward the great lady of steel welcoming them like a mother. And for an instant, I let my mind transport me back in time, decades earlier, when I wasn't even born. To a time when my grandfather had come to this harbor, on his way to the coalmines of West Virginia. The same man who had built the hut I had been conceived, born, and raised in. A man I hadn't even a picture of. And for that man I felt a deep sense of gratitude now, for had it not been for him, perhaps we mightn't have had a roof over our heads. I felt grateful for his courage and strength, qualities that drove millions like him to come to this land.

I imagined him standing on the pier, next to the boat, a *beretta* clasped to his head, holding a battered valise containing all his belongings, looking around him in dismay, lost, not knowing where his next meal would come from. And perhaps wondering where he would sleep after dark, and yet determined to provide for his family. And now, standing on the same soil where a giant of a generation stood before, I felt a strange kinship with this new land under my feet. It was as though I had been part of that same great migration, and I thought of those men and women that came across the vast ocean in rickety boats, and for a moment I dared to share their joy, their secret dreams.

An officer wearing a light green uniform instructed me to join the visitor's line with a flick of his hand. The level of organization was impressive. Everything ran as smoothly and efficiently as a giant machine. But there was a new rhythm that seemed to govern this new world. I could sense it, but couldn't define it. However, on closer observation, it came to me. Everyone seemed to move faster here, like wind-up dolls.

There was a striking frenetic beat that propelled life here, a hurried boiling in the air.

I strode over to a booth and handed my passport to a bald, heavyset officer. He inspected it, glanced at me approvingly, and stamped it. "Welcome to America," he called across the glass counter. I nodded and walked away, savoring each word.

I stood in the immense hall, dazed with excitement and jet lag. A large clock on the wall read 12:45. In Milano it was 6:45 in the evening. I pictured Mama still teary-eyed washing dishes at the sink in her small kitchen; my father sitting in the living room watching a Western on TV; Silvio sitting cross-legged on his bed pouring over his political science books; Mario slung in the brown armchair in the living room, savoring a bite of *gelato*. I pictured the long tile corridor glowing from too much floor wax, cold underfoot even in summer.

Mama wouldn't sleep tonight. She'd toss and turn, then get up, trudge to my room, sit in the chair near the window, a blanket wrapped around her shoulder, and stare into the starless night sky. She'd conjure up images of a distant land, a land which had taken her son away. But perhaps all of this pain, this sorrow she harbored in her heart would be lightened by the thought of a better life lying ahead for all of us. There she'd sit, listening to the loud beating of her heart, to the stillness of the cold night, till she dozed off in the chair, reciting silent Hail Marys.

I'd never been so far away from home. Then the realization hit me. I was on my own now. Home was mine to make. The comforting thought of Al's benevolent smile eased my anxiety.

I'd felt a quick sense of camaraderie with the man in Milano. But above all I'd sensed his purity of heart, and the self-confidence he exuded in all circumstances. That quality that's so American, which I'd discover myself years later.

What if things didn't work out? What then, I thought, a rolling wave of fear and excitement tightening my stomach. Life had taught me plenty of street smarts. And like most men, I could get used to anything. The parsimonious ways I grew up with would allow me to make it on practically nothing. A pan of cooked rice and chick peas drizzled with olive oil could feed me for a week, if need be.

I shook myself loose from these thoughts. No doubt my grandfather was the thread that tied me to this continent. Again, I thought of the man and the only memories I had of him. A few coins from a foreign land, a yellow-wrapped candy, and a few bounces on his bony knee. People said he was a night wanderer, slept only a few hours at dawn, round-faced and red-dimpled cheeks. A fierce older man with a set chin and darting, inquiring eyes. And it was said that he knew everyone's business in the village.

Growing up, I'd heard stories of American soldiers who, during the last world war, had parachuted into our mountain forests by mistake. They dangled from tree branches until the villagers cut them down. The people offered them food, wine, and a place to spend the night. As they left to rejoin their units in the city the next day, those soldiers left behind sugar, chocolate, and American cigarettes as a token of appreciation for the local hospitality. But most of all, they left a legacy of America as the great savior of the world. The local women dismantled their parachutes and reassembled them into beautiful wedding gowns. Several of my aunts had gotten married in these. The gowns were soft and smooth as the rarest silk.

Al had told me that when his father had set foot on this continent, he knelt, kissed the ground, made the sign of the cross with his fingers on the new soil, and swore never to return to his homeland. The man never broke his promise.

There was vitality in the air, and a sense of infinite possibilities in this new land. And the spirit of adventure which had drawn me to it was not diminished by my arrival. I took Uncle Larry's note out of my bag. It read: "To whom it may concern: please help this young man since he doesn't speak English."

I'd met him in Calabria years before. He was a saint of a man who had sent me several pairs of tennis shoes over the years. I wasn't going to wear the note around my neck with a chain as he suggested in his letter. That would be embarrassing. Too bad he lived in Cleveland and couldn't be here to greet me.

I took a good last look at the tall glass gates I'd entered. If there had been a tree, I'd have carved my name on its trunk with my pocket knife, like I used to do in Calabria, so that someday I could return to recapture that special moment. But there wasn't one, so I imprinted in my mind the image of those doors separating two continents, two worlds.

I made my way through the airport to the connecting flight, bombarded by the sounds of an incomprehensible language. I caught a word now and then as I threaded through the crowd.

But for the most part I felt like a drunk stumbling through a snowstorm. Meanwhile, my imagination flew west, to the vast expanses of the Western world I knew from watching American movies. I'd no chance to see what the East looked like, but I sensed that there must be an enormous difference between the two halves of the country. The West, in my eyes, appeared truly wild, with no collective sense of culture, where a man, relying solely on his will and ability, could become anything he set out to be. The West seemed unbound by traditions, free to roam its measureless spaces, and full of possibilities.

When I got off the plane in San Francisco, Al stood out in the crowd of onlookers waiting at the gate. He was an imposing figure in his gray polyester three-piece suit, well-polished black shoes, and spectacles.

"Welcome to California," he called out. He was in his element here, carefree and self-confident. I was about to hug him when his hand reached out for mine. I'd heard that although Americans displayed their emotions in public, like holding hands, cuddling, and even kissing—things I never saw my parents do—they also cherished their privacy and space. Maybe it was just in our family where we were always kissing and hugging like we were going off to war.

We made small talk about the trip as we headed to pick up my suitcase. I removed the black ribbon Mama had tied to the handle to keep the *malocchio*, the evil spirits, at bay before he noticed it. He put the valise in the trunk of his Chrysler New Yorker, and we drove away.

We headed out into the maze of freeways that crossed over and under each other like a swarm of mating snakes. It was difficult to believe the size of cars here, the four- and five-lane roads, and the sense of limitless space. Everything seemed built on a larger scale. Even the sky seemed larger, with its soft hues of gold and pink, the Western sun about to set over the rolling hills. A cold breeze blew in the air. Milano's snow-littered streets came to mind, the pale sky, and the bone-piercing cold.

Soon San Francisco Bay stretched before us. Tall buildings loomed in the distance. San Francisco. The city of the song, perched on the last stretch of land leaning into the Pacific. I had dreamed of this place. The city stood charming and mysterious, like the night. My eyes ready to steal a piece of its allure, I felt like a conquistador nearing a hidden treasure.

"Well, how you like it so far, Peter?"

Was this my new name? It didn't seem to fit me right. I liked the sound of it well enough, but it wasn't really me. Al's eyes blazed with anticipation. This was his land.

"Beautiful," I said, and meant it.

"Well," he nodded as if congratulating himself, "I knew you would like it. I guess you must be tired."

I was, but now the fatigue was leaving me as the adrenaline kicked in. "Not really." I'd no idea what was in store for the evening. "Are we going home now?"

"No." He glanced over again. "I've got some business to take care of in the morning. We'll leave right after."

He had clients in the city and was trying to close a big deal he had been working on for months, he explained. But the whole thing sounded pretty vague to me, and not interesting at all. But he seemed anxious about it. An engineer, he dealt in industrial glass.

Al parked the car against the curb of a steep hill, and for a moment I thought the automobile would tip over. When we got out of the car, a colder breeze swept over us. I could hear various Italian dialects as people rushed in and out of little shops and sauntered down busy, glittering streets. The place reminded me of Milano. The aromas of the nearby ocean and of freshly baked bread floated in the air. White houses crowded around us. Light strands of fog rolled in, drifted slowly over the streets, and in places hung like veils. Titillating aromas of food seeped out of small shops' doors as we passed.

We walked up a couple more blocks and entered a restaurant. The aroma of fried fish engulfed us as we walked through the door. It was a loud, long, narrow space that reminded me of the *trattorie* in Milano. A waiter showed us to a small table, handed us a couple of menus, and left.

The city was difficult to visualize. It seemed to be laid out on more than one hill. Scenes from *Bullitt* with Steve McQueen replayed on the screen of my imagination. I asked Al where we were.

He looked up from his menu and took off his spectacles. "Oh, this here is North Beach," he said. "Lots of Italians live here, and the food is great."

The menu was mostly fish. Al suggested the *cioppino*—a combination of seafood sautéed in a light tomato sauce, typical of southern Italy—and the fried calamari, his favorite appetizer. He leaned over the table. "They are fried just right, not overcooked or soggy with oil." He certainly was right. When the waiter brought them to the table they were golden and puffed, served with lemon wedges and sprinkled with minced parsley and a hint of fresh garlic to enhance *il sapore*.

I stared out at the tall, misty downtown buildings dressed in their night-lights. Little bright stars shone like diamonds in the western sky. Church bells rang close by. The image of my village with its church above the riverbank flashed in my head. It seemed a million miles away now. A strange but pleasant feeling stirred in me as I gazed out the window. The many nationalities inhabiting this land were still overwhelming. It seemed as if the whole world congregated out in the streets. And thinking of Al's enormous Chrysler New Yorker down the street confirmed the infinite possibilities of this new world.

"Want to take a ride around the city?" Al suggested.

I thought he would never ask.

The orange steel towers of the Golden Gate looked like giants keeping vigil. The bridge was breathtaking up close, while the lights of oncoming cars glaring in the misty night painted an almost surreal picture. Al began to give me dates, names, and figures on the many facets of its construction history; he was an engineer, after all. I tuned him out and basked in the beauty of the city of lights, and this bridge of dreams.

From the hotel balcony strings of lights glowed over the city and out into the bay. And as I stood on the balcony, hands gripping the rail, the cold wind tousling my hair, I could feel a wave of excitement slowly rise inside my chest. It seemed the Far West had been waiting for me all along.

After the eleven o'clock news, I changed the time on my watch, and left the Old World behind.

Departure day at Malpensa airport. My uncle Frank to my left, relatives to my right.

CALAMARI FRITTI

DEEP-FRIED SQUID

Serves 4-5 as appetizers.

3 lbs of squid	2 tablespoons of chopped Italian parsley
1 teaspoon of fresh minced garlic(optional)	1 cup of all-purpose flour
Vegetable oil	6 lemon wedges, and salt to taste

Detach the tentacles from the body of the squid in the kitchen sink. Cut the head below the eyes and discard. (Unless you want to squeeze and collect the black ink and color fresh pasta with it.) Remove the beak from the tentacles. Remove long bone from inside the squid. Wash freely under cold running water, removing and discarding inside matter from squid. Cut squid into ½ inch rings. Pat dry with paper towels. However, today you can find nearly cleaned squid almost anywhere. (Usually frozen, in small one lb packs.) This saves you lots of tedious work.

Fill a heavy, medium-size skillet about halfway with vegetable oil. Use a saucepan for safety if children are around. Place over high heat. Drop a handful of squid onto a platter with the flour. Mix and coat well. Transfer squid into a sieve. Shake well to remove excess flour.

When the oil is very hot, and you begin to almost see wisps of smoke rise, cautiously lower the squid into the oil. Be careful not to crowd the pan. Fry the squid until it is puffed and golden, about 60 seconds. Remove with a slotted spoon, place on paper towels to drain. When all the squid have been fried, set them on a large warm platter, sprinkle with parsley, garlic, and salt to taste, garnish with lemon wedges, and serve at once. I like mine with a squeeze of lemon.

If you overcook squid, they will taste rubbery. If the oil isn't very hot, they will be soggy.

ELEVEN

The city shined in the early morning hours. Although it had lost some of its night charm and luster, it was still beautiful. The massive Bay Bridge seemed to be within reach of my outstretched hand. I cherished this moment in a sort of meditative silence. As Al drove around tight corners and busy streets, I basked in San Francisco like a bird in the sun. There hadn't been too many happy moments in my life. It had been a constant struggle to have the ordinary things other people took for granted. The provincial life had made me resentful, yet profoundly appreciative of every good thing that came my way. To be here, in awe of this city I had heard so much about, humbled me.

I could smell baking bread and strong whiffs of espresso floating in the North Beach air. The city's night postcard look gone, it teemed with life now. The clusters of white houses seemed ready to tumble over, and gazing up at them provoked an unsteady feeling in my head. The sight of struggling trolleys climbing up the steep hillsides like tired beetles toward the sky was fascinating. I pictured Milano waking up to a new day, trams lines scampering everywhere, deep lines of people standing at café counters drinking cappuccino and espresso before heading to work.

Past midday, as we drove down the crowded city streets of Chinatown, with its glistening roasted ducks hanging outside show windows, the pungent aromas of the mysterious Orient floated in the air.

After Al concluded his business, we drove over the Bay Bridge. It was mind-boggling to ride over such an imposing structure of steel and cement as it flew over the blue waters of the bay. In the rearview mirror I could see the city behind us shrinking. A sense of loss gripped me, as if I was leaving behind someone dear.

Soon a fertile valley rose into view. Al seemed in his element as he listened to the news and tapped the steering wheel, eyes glued to the road ahead. The valley grew wider and deeper, its black and brown soils rich and fertile.

"Well?" said Al, as soon as the news was over and he turned off the radio. "How you like it so far?"

I laughed and nodded. "How much farther?"

Al looked at his gold wristwatch. "Three more hours." He raised three fingers.

The distances here were difficult to believe, considering you could drive from Milano to Firenze in less than two hours.

"Did you sleep well?" Al asked.

"Yes, I did."

Some of my English exercises from the Institute popped up in my head now and again, but for the most part we spoke *dialetto Calabrese*.

The road stretched ahead, endless and wide, as the big car sailed along quiet and smooth, its tires singing their muffled tune against the pavement. Plains stretched before us in all directions. It was like a sea of land. Watching the way the golden light fell and spread over the rolling hills, the grazing black and brown cattle, and the vast farms, I realized that I had arrived in the West of my childhood imagination.

Before long Al exited the freeway and drove down a country road and into a gas station. A sign at a corner read "Fresno." I had seen the name of the town on the map. But besides open plains and a few tall, distant buildings southward, there wasn't much more. The air felt warm and flat. I took off my jacket, tossed it in the back seat, and loosened my tie, as an omnipotent sun flooded the fields.

As I studied the plains around me, I wondered where the world I had seen in countless western movies had gone. The endless prairies were around me just as I had envisioned, but where were the cowboys? The Indians? What kind of West could be without them? I thought, perplexed.

An interminable cargo train lumbered in the distance. It huffed and puffed, its whistle shrieking. It spewed puffs of black smoke that curled and lingered behind as the centipede of steel advanced. As the train got closer, rattling and thumping, I could read an insignia in bold white letters: *Santa Fe*.

"There," I whispered to myself. "There goes a piece of the Old West."

My eyes followed the train as it trundled down tracks that cut a straight path through fields of rippling green grass. And when the train passed from sight, I realized that a world had passed with it. It was gone now, alive only in my imagination and on film stock.

But despite this disappointment, there was a country charm in the air that made me feel at home. Land and open spaces make my heart swell every time. And in comparison to the hustle and bustle of Milano, this seemed like paradise. No traffic, congestion, or the roaring torrent of madness that spills out of a city at rush hour. Here, if I listened closely, I may have heard the faint breath of the land itself pulsating beneath my feet.

From the moment I stepped off the plane, the signs of the excess and abundance of America had glared at me. And the gas station we stopped at on the way into Fresno was no exception. Although it was a faded, peeling white and gray wooden shack, the inside was amazingly modern and functional. Its shelves brimmed with unfamiliar merchandise, including plenty of matches displayed inside a little wicker basket on the front counter. Free matches! This blew me away. In Italy they were a monopoly item. I had already accumulated a collection from various establishments under Al's dismayed eye.

The other sign of excess was the huge canopy covering the four gas pumps outside. I chuckled, thinking of the tiny gasoline vendors along the curbs in Milano. These *Americani* did things on a grand scale.

The gas tank filled, we got in the car and got back onto the highway. "You hungry, Peter?"

I was.

Downtown Fresno seemed deserted in comparison to Milano's center. Weren't there supposed to be people walking the streets in America? When I asked him, Al gave out a roaring laugh. He explained that hardly anyone walked the streets in these parts. The news stunned me.

In minutes we pulled into a parking lot next to a motorcycle shop. The scent of crisp baking dough and tomato sauce permeated the midday air. A neon sign shaped like Italy hung above a restaurant door. In a foreign landscape, such a familiar sight seemed out of place, yet it drew me in like an old acquaintance. "A nice *Abruzzese* family owns it—a clan of brothers," Al said.

An open kitchen sat beyond a counter lined with red-topped stools. "*O sole mio*" blared from speakers nestled in the corners. The aromas of tomato sauce, fried onions, and baking bread filled the air in the long and cozy dining room. Al suggested the calzone and the veal scaloppini. When the meal arrived I couldn't believe the size of the fried and puffed calzone. It was gargantuan. But then, everything else was bigger in America. Why should the food be any different?

As we headed south on highway ninety-nine, the valley glowed greener. Vineyards extended as far as the eye could see, along with plots of almond trees in bloom. It was as if nature knew how to attract attention with her beauty.

I wondered what these relatives were like, and the prospect of sharing my life with them made me a bit anxious. But from Al's behavior I knew I'd be welcomed and safe. Al seemed like a best friend, an element missing between my father and me.

The big car glided along toward the mountains, home to the small town of Exeter, past thick clusters of orange and olive groves, rock-strewn hills, and grassy slopes where cattle grazed placidly under a cloudless sky. Before long, a low, square building emerged into view. Al eased the car off the road, entered the driveway, and came to a stop.

I walked to the edge of the building, arching my sore back. The little valley huddled low as it stretched toward the foothills. With the road on one side and the foothills on the other, it seemed tucked in like a baby in a cradle.

The hilltops were strewn with massive rocks. Lonely pine trees stood vigil over the wild landscape. In the valley below, a brown house sat inside a patch of oak trees a couple hundred yards away. A swimming pool in back of the house glittered in the sun. A half dozen black cattle grazed in a corral adjoining the unpaved road. The rich smell of fresh tilled soil drifted to me. Al put his hand on my shoulder. "This is God's country, my dear boy." He gazed and nodded proudly at his kingdom. If there was paradise on earth, this spot was it. We stood there in silence, staring at the dotted yellow plains of mustard fields stretching before us.

I was given a warm welcome.

The moon held a finger to her lips and smiled. The little valley lay peaceful and resting under the brilliance of her silver glow. Somewhere in the distance a dog barked once. An automobile rumbled by on the dark highway. A deep silence hovered over the sleeping plains as I stared out the open window of my room that night. I pictured my family asleep in Milano. Was Mama all right? Or was she awake, in my room, sitting before her sewing machine, teary-eyed next to the red bookcase, stitching her sorrows away? I pondered my new life. I was thousands of miles away from home at only twenty. It amazed me that desire had gotten me this far.

CALZONE BASIC PIZZA DOUGH

Serves 2

1 1/2 cups of unbleached all-purpose flour

1 package dry yeast, stirred and activated in half cup of lukewarm water

2 tablespoons olive oil

1 teaspoon salt

1 beaten egg

Fresh dough can also be purchased at most delis, if you like to avoid making it yourself.

Combine yeast, water, oil, and salt in a medium-size bowl. Whisk well. Add flour and mix well by hand until blended. Transfer the dough to a work surface and knead 5 to 6 minutes until smooth and pliable. If sticky, dust it with flour and knead it a bit longer. Place the dough into a large bowl, cover with plastic wrap, and let it rise in a lukewarm place for close to an hour and a half. During this time, the dough should double in volume—if it doesn't, let it rest a little longer.

Preheat oven to 375.

Calzone Filling

In a bowl, combine:

8 oz ricotta cheese	**2 tablespoons grated Pecorino cheese**
6 oz diced mozzarella	
	1 egg
6-8 oz diced salami, cooked sausage, or prosciutto (your choice.)	**Salt to taste**

Mix all ingredients. Mixture should be uniform and not too dry or soft. Divide the dough into two equal parts. Stretch by hand or with rolling pin two circles of about 6 to 7 inches in diameter. Place half of the filling in the center of each circle. Fold the dough over and press closed at the edges. Then seal the edges all around with the tines of a fork.

Place the calzones on a baking sheet lightly coated with oil. Brush each calzone with beaten egg. Bake for about 10 to 12 minutes till golden. Serve hot or lukewarm.

TWELVE

Soon Al and his wife filed the necessary forms to change my tourist visa to foreign student status, which allowed me to remain legally in the country.

I enrolled in a night English course at the College of the Sequoias in Visalia. I rode along with my cousin Charles, Al's older boy, in his Jeep. He was one of those very bright boys that seemed to live in the academic stratosphere—a calculus genius who made me feel like I'd been born with a bird's brain. I'd been a disaster in math throughout my school years, and had never heard of calculus.

The campus was made up of a compact set of two-story buildings painted a mint green color to match with the theme, I assumed, of Sequoia National Park in the nearby Sierra Nevada mountains. My beginners' English class was held on the lower floor of one of the campus buildings. It was populated by foreigners like me, most of whom erroneously believed they spoke very good English. I could hardly make out a word they said. But the consolation was that I felt like I was rubbing elbows with the whole world. From my desk, peering between the window's plastic blinds, I could see cars sailing down Mooney Boulevard, the town's major thoroughfare. And that's where my mind used to hover for most of the classes, taking refuge from the twists and turns of the English language. I felt like I was in an auditory fog, where only unintelligible sounds reached my ears. And despite my cousin's patient and careful enunciation of each short sentence, the world remained a blur to me. Those long months seem to be the darkest, most frustrating period of my life in America.

This was also the time when I began to miss my native food. Pasta, salami, prosciutto, crunchy golden bread, cheese, cappuccino, espresso—all items my body craved. I particularly missed bread. I couldn't believe that spongy stuff that was sold in supermarkets pretending to pass for the substance of life. Not even if I had dentures could I submit to such an insult. And no matter how hard I tried to comply with civility every morning at the breakfast table, I couldn't force down the pancakes drizzled with honey, fried eggs and small links of glistening sausage that greeted me. Used to a simple croissant and a cappuccino as my breakfast, my body simply refused to adapt to this new regimen.

Milling around with the foreign contingent in exile on the campus grounds, I discovered that a vast majority of students lived on their own or shared an apartment with a roommate or two. Somehow, this seemed the most appealing arrangement in the world to me. This was part of the sense of freedom and easy accessibility of comforts America was renowned for. A few months later, when I told my relatives I intended to live on my own, they were disappointed by my decision. I sensed it was best for me to find a new sponsor, and avoid family friction and disagreement.

I was tired of drawing stares everywhere I went in my tailored Italian suit, so I bought myself a black cowboy hat, a red and blue checkered shirt, and a pair of brown leather boots. I inspected myself in the shop's mirror. *There*, I thought. *Now I fit in.*

Al's mother, meanwhile, keeping up with southern Italian traditions, had been trying to marry me off to an Italian girl in southern California with whom they were very well acquainted. I wasn't fond of such conjugal maneuvers, although I'd been exposed to such nonsense all my life. I wanted to be my own person, make my own decisions, particularly regarding these delicate matters. And besides, the world was no longer in the Dark Ages. However, Aunt Mary, gifted with her subtle smile and diplomatic manners, was quick to point out that sooner or later I'd have to consider marrying someone. That was, if I wanted to stay in America, and get my "Green Card." I'd no idea what that was. Or if it was green. She was insistent, and finally I gave in to the idea. In all fairness, who knew what life could bring my way. In addition, deep in me there was a mild curiosity to see what the girl looked like. Most men harbor these feelings. Even if the idea of marriage sends them running like startled birds, they can't resist the allure of a woman. I corresponded with the young woman for months, and later ended up in

Indio with her family as my new sponsor. Sadly, although she was pleasant to look at, nothing romantic ever blossomed between us.

I was offered a job as assistant cook in her family's restaurant, Ciro's, off Highway 111. Indio, a tiny town in the Coachella Valley, compared with Milano, or even Fresno, seemed perched at the edge of the world. It made up for its bleakness, however, with the beauty and grandeur of the desert, with its ivory sandy dunes and colorful wildflowers that framed the town like a painting. The restaurant was more of a pizzeria, with a simple menu of basic pasta dishes like cannelloni, manicotti, and spaghetti with meatballs. But the pizzas, medium thick, were so good that when you bit into the golden crust, your mouth sang with a melody of flavors.

Overly protective of their Neapolitan family recipe, they made each daily batch of dough in the back of the restaurant in complete secrecy. No one was allowed to approach. Making pizza was serious business to them, an art brought over from the Old World. It was strictly forbidden to use a rolling pin to flatten the dough. You had to do it by hand, stretch it with your fingertips, flip it in the air for showmanship. They served well over a hundred pizzas per day. Working behind hot stoves and ovens when the temperature outside reached 113 degrees, however, seemed suicidal. This was the first time I realized how hard people worked in this country, how thirstily they chased after success. In America it seemed people lived to work, whereas Italians merely worked to live.

Despite my language difficulties and the painful adjustment to a life that offered very little social interaction, a new transformation began taking place in me. I wanted to feel in charge of my own destiny, and there seemed to be no better place in the world to accomplish this than America.

After two long years of thumbing my way to school and back every day, I bought my first car, a used white Rambler station wagon. I paid a hundred and forty-nine dollars for it. It had coffee-stained leather seats and a luggage rack, and it leaked oil. But the engine was sound, and with a little work it had the potential to become quite fast. I remembered my old bicycle, and felt like a rich man.

The graduation ceremony gave me goose bumps. Standing in line to receive my diploma, wearing the traditional black gown and cap, I felt for the first time as though I were a citizen of this new culture. The elaborate event was a stunning experience, and it couldn't have been more American, I thought. By then, the desert had grown to be like an old friend. There was a mysterious energy to it that has remained with me to this day. And when on a late August morning I drove away to go to school in the Central Valley, I almost had tears in my eyes.

Then I cut through the glittering sea of sand, watching the leaves of palm trees sway in the morning breeze in my rearview mirror. And as the desert receded, my life stretched ahead unbounded, offering infinite possibilities. In a few weeks it would be my birthday: twenty-three. And life had never seemed so carefree and good. It seemed as if it would last forever.

Earning a degree in American literature at Fresno State was a challenge, for I still didn't have a full command of the language. However, this was also the most propitious and fruitful period of my intellectual development. Free to think only of myself, I plunged into the school curriculum with such a fervor that I absorbed knowledge like a sponge, sensing that a time like this would probably never come again.

I got a job at Di Cicco's on Abby and Belmont Avenue, making pizza and their football-sized *calzone*. Restaurant work was easy, and the hours short. On weekend nights, when I got off work around eleven, I would get into my souped-up Rambler, which awaited me out in the parking lot behind the restaurant next to a giant eucalyptus tree. I'd spent a considerable sum to bring its weary engine up to speed. I don't know exactly what my friend the mechanic had done to it. But it sounded mean, and that's all I cared about. The exterior was still quite nice—one of those pristine whites that shined after a good wash. There were no major dents, only a few almost invisible scratches that ran along the passenger side, which no one could notice at night. Brand new steel-belted tires with shiny hubcaps gave it a flair of subdued elegance, contrasting nicely with its paint. The only eyesore, which I contemplated removing often, was its long luggage rack.

After a quick inspection in the rearview mirror to smooth out my looks, I'd light a cigarette, and then slowly maneuver my way out of the parking lot and onto the side street north of the Harley Davison shop. From there, cautiously, I'd veer left onto Blackstone Avenue, a one-way street. And just about thirty feet up, I'd merge into the full flow of the cruising river of throbbing engines that paraded up and down Belmont Avenue like a swarm of drone bees, at less than ten miles per hour. Cigarette dangling from my mouth, elbow resting on the window's ledge, adrenaline kicking in at the sight of some of the most beautiful girls my eyes had ever seen, I'd join the parade, feeling as though I were in one of those James Dean movies.

Belmont and Blackstone Avenue were the epicenter of the world on weekends then. This was where youth pulsated with longing hearts. Life flowed unbounded here, like the sea. And there I was in the midst of it all, soaking in every nuance, every furtive glance tossed my way, every flirtatious smile. It was exciting to be part of the last real migration of teenagers cruising the streets of town. I'd unknowingly caught the tail end of an era in American life, which by the end of the seventies would become only a memory. Most nights I wasn't so lucky. Some nights I was downright offended. Rowdy girls with beer bottles and cigarettes in hand would lean out the windows of their boyfriends' thundering cars, displaying their provocative tank tops, and ask me, "So, where did you leave Grandma tonight?" What a blow. I'd been thinking I was so cool.

On nights like these, when my pride had sunk to low ebb, I'd pull off into the Big Boy burger joint on the corner. There, I'd order a burger, then sink into the soft burgundy booth, downtrodden.

Later, I'd drive to the mountains. I'd ease north on Blackstone Avenue with its glaring lights spilling onto the street, past Shaw Avenue, where another crowd usually convened outside in the other Big Boy parking lot. From there I'd ease past the UA movie house, and down into Pinedale. Here I always slowed to admire the little western-fronted shops, and then exited the town on 41, crossing the San Joaquin River, past walnut and olive groves, and across rustling plains that slept under the starry sky. I drove up the winding two-lane highway through the mountains. Sometimes slowing to let a deer cross the road, I listened to the mysterious sounds of the night, and smelled the scent of pine.

I'd drive on in the pitch darkness, the car's headlights illuminating the trunks of redwood trees and jackrabbits with glinting yellow eyes that leapt across the road. The cool mountain breeze would blow through my hair, while the night hovered quiet and sweet.

I would sit on the shore of Shaver Lake, my knees drawn to my chest, and stare at the moon's undulating reflection in the water. Steeped in silence, I watched night come, startled occasionally by the whispers of the woods, the gentle night wind. This spot reminded me of Chiavenna, where Uncle and I used to hunt for porcini mushrooms in the fall.

Chiavenna is a small town nestled in the high mountains, only a few kilometers from the Swiss border where we spent many summer Sundays. It was an idyllic place as a getaway from the smog and congestion of Milano. The beautiful sight of Lake Como kept us company like a silent friend as we drove the serpentine road. In the majestic mountains porcini grew in frantic abundance after the first rainy season in October. Uncle and I used to roam the lush woods for hours on end, plastic bags dangling from our wrists, eyes alert like hunters after prey. We scoured every inch of ground in search of that elusive yellowish cap protruding inches above damp soil. It truly felt like a treasure hunt every time luck struck and presented us with a coveted glimpse of a few porcini camouflaging themselves like soldiers ready to launch an ambush. As though they were waiting, hoping no eyes would notice their disguise. Fingers gently removing debris from their moist caps, we would eye each other with profound satisfaction at our catch. The soft, damp porcini lying in the palms of our hands brought forth the scent of its life-giving mother, the mountain.

That alone made our day.

Nearly five years in this country, and I still marveled at the vastness of this land. Beyond these mountains were lakes, valleys, paved black roads that shimmered in the afternoon sun like melting lead. Roads that had been forged out of pure determination, and loss of lives, following the tracks of the pioneer wagons that had inched across an untamed continent. Endless roads moved across the measureless West, and connected the entire country.

During school I met Jane. Romance simmered. After graduation in the late seventies, I took her to Milano to introduce her to my family and marry. But due to our cultural differences, things soon turned sour, and a few days later she returned to America.

For weeks, I lingered in Milano feeling sorry for myself. Mama told me to stop moaning and get over it, and not to consider getting serious over a foreign woman again, for no foreign woman would put up with my old-world ways. I think perhaps Mama was glad I hadn't married after all, so that she could still take comfort in the idea I hadn't left the family. This was only a hunch, but it sometimes flared in the back of my mind when I thought about Jane.

I got a job as a pizza and grill man at the Boccaccio restaurant on the French Riviera to brush up on my French and expand my cooking skills. I rented a dismal *mansarde* in the old part of town, at Rue de la Prefecture 17, and discovered that by poking my head out a hole in the roof I could see the entire town of Nice. The restaurant was an elegant establishment located in the glitzy and busy Rue Massena, a few blocks from a posh casino. It offered wood-oven pizza, fresh-grilled seafood, and many French dishes like *bouillabaisse* and *côte de boeuf*.

The chef was a temperamental man with dark, brooding eyes who rarely saw humor in life. He ruled over his kitchen with an iron hand as he and his three young assistants churned out elaborate entrées. I tried gaining his confidence to learn some of his recipes, but he made it clear he wasn't interested in my stories about America. Passing through the kitchen, I observed a very interesting technique I had never seen before: tossing individual portions of pre-cooked pasta into skillets containing specific sauces to let the pasta absorb the sauce's flavor for a couple of minutes before it was served.

At night, after I got off work, most of the gang from the restaurant, cooks and waiters alike, escorted the boss to the casino to play his nightly roulette game. Like a bunch of vultures, we stood around the posh table sipping from our drinks. We watched the golden wheel of fortune spin and spin into the late hours of the night.

Later, I'd stroll down Promenade des Anglais listening to the whispers of the Mediterranean Sea breaking softly on the white sand shore and feeling the deep emptiness Jane had left in my heart. I longed to see her.

Some nights, I was hurled back to America by memories of the San Joaquin Valley. The grand life of the French Riviera seemed insignificant in comparison. There seemed to be no more idyllic place than the San Joaquin Valley—the Sierra Nevada, the cool, blue water of Shaver Lake in full summer, the charming, dusty little towns on the fringes of Fresno that expire after sundown. And from a continent away, thinking of that microcosm, a feeling of happiness lifted my heart. All of these reactions were partially colored by the image of Jane that floated before my eyes.

I worked in Nice for five months, then I went back to my family in Milano. It felt good to be back in Europe after almost five years. I had realized that my little country was highly regarded in the world. Italy had contributed so much art and history, yet I'd taken it all for granted. I reawakened to the people and places of my homeland, and rediscovered the pleasure of listening to the sweet sounds of my native language. I even caught up with old friends from school. Most of them were married with families now. They seemed happy. They didn't complain about their mundane lives. They seemed comfortable, secure in their own little worlds. I wondered why I'd been so different, why I'd left, and what I'd gained. I envied their complacency because they probably never questioned their own motives. I'd been cultivating my thoughts all my life, and I'd ended up not knowing who I'd become. I felt like a composite of two worlds. I'd made myself the son of two countries, an unsettled soul hovering between two continents. And the irony of it all was that a void still lay buried in me—a void I had no idea how to fill.

I wondered whether I'd ever be happy.

During the time I was in America, Grandfather had died. He had only been in his late sixties, but he had smoked three packs of Murattis a day. Growing up, I used to steal two or more cigarettes a day from his pack. From the doorway, sometimes, I'd spy on him as he stood examining the pack in his hand, his graying eyebrows raised in mild suspicion,

158

possibly wondering whether the years were affecting his memory.

I went to the cemetery and laid white orchids on his tomb. I thought about all the fishing trips we had gone on on the river Po over the years, Grandfather riding his white Guzzi while I clasped him from behind on the short leather seat, the wind blowing in our faces, the fishing rods vibrating in my hand. Or the hunting trips we took along the marshes of the river Po, where *storni* were plentiful, nestled atop cottonwood trees, hiding under thick brush. Many times I became the hunting dog, fetching the birds out of their hiding places for Grandfather. He had turned out all right, after all. He'd loved me more than I ever expected, more than I could have asked for. And as I stood there, I seemed to hear a faint celestial music rising from somewhere. Maybe it was his spirit lifting from the earth, telling me again that music never dies, like he often used to say.

I couldn't resist revisiting my old neighborhood.

It hadn't changed. In America, a shopping center would be leveled off, and in the next few weeks a high-rise would take its place. The changes here were imperceptible. It was as though time had stopped. A few of the buildings had new facades or windows, or a different color of paint, but otherwise the neighborhood had changed little. I stood outside by the street corner and watched in dismay. The spot where I used to lean the bicycle against the wall was empty now, as though time had swallowed those moments, days, and years. Slowly, I gazed up at the light burgundy five-story building above the shop and realized I'd never really seen it. I'd never taken the time to look at it in the bustle of every day. I wondered how many things I'd looked at in my life, and never really seen.

The restaurant across the street where Uncle and I used to lunch, and where the idea to become a cook first occurred to me, was now a hardware store. The great white oak trees flanking the long boulevard and the tram tracks had grown, their trunks thicker, branches longer. The transit system had been revamped. The trams and buses had changed from their old dark green to a bright new orange.

I stood watching customers go in and out of the butcher shop for a long time. I watched expectantly as though I were looking to see my old self exit, white jacket stained red with blood, plastic bag in hand, heading for my bicycle as Uncle stood in the doorway, smoke puffing from his nostrils, telling me to hurry. And although I could hear his muffled voice in my head, neither one of us materialized. Uncle was working at a new butcher shop now.

The café next door, where Uncle used to play poker while I daydreamed of America, was still there. But there were no flashy cars parked by the curb anymore, no strutting pimps caressing the thick rolls of cash in their pockets. I waited a little longer, then left.

I even managed a quick trip down to Calabria. I hadn't been there in more than twenty years. Most of my relatives and friends were gone now. Some had emigrated to Australia, others to northern Italy in search of a better life, while others had died. And what remained in the village were old people, cats, and stray dogs.

Our house was—well, the walls. The roof had caved in, and what was left now were the bare, crumbling walls. It looked like a skeleton of rubble, not a house anymore, the house where my brothers used to play on the floor. I stood outside, watching the sagging, cracked wooden door still hanging from its rusty hinges, the patches of overgrown moss in the corner where my bed once sat, old birds' nests on a wooden beam, and a kitten basking in the sun on the chipped front steps, grass in the crevices, where I used to sit staring at the sunset, the mountains, and the stars. I stood there dazed, aching, remembering that once this place was my whole world, my reason for living, for dreaming.

The poplar tree was gone. It had been cut down for firewood, the toothless old woman clad in a long black dress next door explained when I enquired about it. Then she inspected me from head to toe suspiciously, her little pale eyes scrutinizing me, and she asked who was I looking for, who was I. I smiled and told her. "Oh, my," she said, squinting, looking into my eyes, reaching out with her trembling hand for mine. "Oh my," she repeated, as she shook her veiled head, stroked my hand, hollered her daughter's name.

Back in Milano, things had changed after Grandfather's passing. The house where once I had to wait in line to use the bathroom was now occupied only by Nonna and uncle Frank—both my aunts had moved into their own apartments, leaving them alone. It didn't seem like the old place, full of life, arguments, music, friends, relatives that dropped by at all hours of the day, and which never allowed me a moment of quietness. Without my brothers and I, the house seemed like a convalescent home now. Quiet. Somber. Dark. Nonna kept the wooden shutters lowered halfway, as if mourning the loss of so much life which once had flooded that home.

Italy hadn't changed much during the years I was gone. The bureaucratic monster was still alive and well, particularly when it came to business, which was heavily regulated by the government. Getting a license to open a new business, for instance, took months, sometimes years. Not to mention the long list of documents necessary to process the application. America was decades ahead in this regard.

However I'd changed much during my five years in America, at times it still seemed as though I'd never left home and was merely awakening from a long dream. I'd grown used to the vast open spaces, the comforts, the efficiency, and the easier life. And even if I could hear the faint voices of my past drawing me back to my land, my people, my roots, there was little chance I'd ever return to the place I once called home. America had gotten under my skin.

So what was I searching for here? Even as a boy sitting in the branches of the poplar tree staring at the chain of jagged mountains, I had ached for my life to mean more.

A year later, despite Mama's pleas, I returned to America. By this time my brothers, Silvio and Mario, had come to California. Shortly after, in eighty-one, Mario and I had a short stint at running a restaurant in San Diego. It was my first taste of operating my own business. I cherished the idea of working on my own. But a year later, unappreciated and underpaid, we left.

I spent the next year in Hanford cooking for my dear friend Giuseppe Silvestre, a successful self-made immigrant. Then, restless and dissatisfied again, I returned to Italy and worked in several restaurants in Milano, developing a style of cuisine I could call my own. By now, despite many difficulties and disappointments, I'd no more doubts that this was what I wanted to do.

The last establishment I worked for was a small restaurant a couple of blocks from the Duomo, a baroque cathedral that took over two hundred years to build. It was a massive marble structure, with statues of saints mounted atop each of the ten eighty-foot pillars that supported each of the four facades. It was the symbol of the city, the pride of the Milanesi. Every morning on my way to work, as I went past and glanced up at it, my heart fluttered at the imposing architecture. I remembered the days when I had cut school to wander its slanted marble roofs under the gaze of the gold Madonna that crowns its cupola. I marveled at the detailed artwork in the maze of intricate passageways, the perfect symmetry of each pillar, statue, nook and cranny, and wondered how such a monumental project was ever accomplished at that time.

In this restaurant in the shadow of the Duomo, every ingredient was fresh from local vendors and markets. Each morning the owner and I made the rounds and loaded the back of his Fiat with crisp produce, porcini, meat, poultry, fish, and bags of piping hot bread from the *panettiere*. This man was the most meticulous chef I ever met, demanding that there be no veins in the meat and no blemishes on the seafood. The fruits for his *macedonia di frutta*, diced seasonal fruits flavored with Grand Marnier and served chilled, had to be flawless.

Here I learned the joy of cooking hearty peasant food, particularly pasta. It was under the tutelage of this tall, blue-eyed, spare Milanese man that I learned the simplicity of combining three or four ingredients to make a beautiful pasta dish. "Remember that simplicity is the best policy when it comes to food," chef Andrea often said. "The freshness of the ingredients and the high quality of products will always yield an excellent cuisine. Food should never be embellished to show customers how well you can draw intricate designs on their plates. Treat food with respect and simplicity, and it will thank you with its flavor."

Andrea also taught me to make *focaccia* and beef and fish stocks; how to grill fish, meat, and vegetables. And he opened my eyes to an endless array of appetizers, including grilled baby octopus, *crostini*, and *carpaccio*. The variety was mind-boggling. The restaurant was busy with customers rushing out of offices in waves and bursting through the doors as soon as we opened for business. Exhausted at the end of the night,

I'd ride the metro home. There I'd decipher the scribbles I'd made in my tiny notebook, recollecting the ingredients of a particular dish, and the proper order of executing it.

But above all, here I learned to cook pasta properly. "Use a tall pot to cook pasta in," Andrea began on my first day on the job. "Pour salt in only when the water has come to a full boil. Put the pasta in it right away, otherwise the salt will oxidize, affecting the pasta's flavor. If available, use Sicilian rock salt—it adds much more flavor. Cook pasta *al dente*. Never rinse pasta under cold water: You will be cursed for eternity for this sin."

At last I felt I'd gained sufficient restaurant experience to feel confident in opening my own business. The idea provoked in me intense excitement, and fear. I'd done a fine job working for other people. Why shouldn't I be able to do it for myself, and reap the benefits? Wasn't this what the American dream was all about? Wasn't this what billionaire Paul Getty was quoted saying once? Choose a field of interest, work in that field a few years, learn as much as possible about the business, and then make the leap on your own. I knew that anyone with average intelligence could make money, if that was what they wanted. I never wanted money for its own sake, but the hard experience of my upbringing left deep scars below the level of my consciousness. Poverty can be a powerful motivator. And it was solely to keep this fear at bay that I sought my own business. True, there was a self-validation factor involved as well. But a small one. And in the billionaire's advice lay my path to the dream of financial freedom. Or so I thought.

As the winter of eighty-three drew near, the bright California sun drew me to America again. As always, Mama tearfully begged me to stay home. I promised her that soon she and Father would join us in California.

MACEDONIA DI FRUTTA

MIXED SEASONAL FRUIT DESSERT

Serves 4

All fruits should be medium ripe.

2 bananas	*2 apples*
2 peaches	*2 kiwis*
2 pears	*granulated sugar and fresh-squeezed juice of a lemon*

Remove skin and cores from apples, pears, and peach. Cut fruits in half, julienne them. Dice strips into cubes ½ inch in diameter, and set in a medium-size bowl. Remove skin and follow same procedure with banana and kiwi. Add 2 oz granulated sugar and the juice of a lemon. Stir and adjust accordingly. Cover bowl with plastic wrap. Stow in refrigerator for about two hours. Serve cold into fruit glasses. A little fresh whipped cream sprinkled with cinnamon might not be such a bad idea, and Savoiardi are excellent on the side.

You may use a larger variety of fruits according to taste and season. Be judicious, however—if you use blueberries, raspberries, or strawberries, they will tint the entire batch. If you must, add them a few minutes before serving.

THIRTEEN

Cupertino, California, 1987

"Pieroo." The manager's voice trailed faintly into the kitchen, nearly drowned out by the chatter in the boisterous dining room. I turned around. "Del Monaco on line two." Joe held up two fingers. I could see him standing by the register through the arches of the long dish-up counter. A group of customers huddled nearby, waiting to be seated. Gigliola, one of the food servers, was offering them hot focaccia bread from a wicker basket lined with a red napkin to pacify them—a great strategy in the business.

Damn. Right in the middle of rush hour. This is going to fuck up the whole evening.

It had been a steady night. Customers had trickled in at a nice even pace. It was good working like this. You could take your time and make sure each order was perfect before it went out. There were four of us on the line that weekend. Alfredo, my *sous* chef, was on the grill. He was a reliable workhorse, loyal and proud like the Aztec blood that ran in his veins. On the pizza oven, at the other end of the line, stood Chui, a wiry, lanky boy of twenty who seemed to live in a perpetual state of agitation. I'd recently promoted him from dishwasher upon discovering he knew the ingredients of every dish in the house. That spoke volumes about the kid's ambition.

And then there was Mario. He was the fastest and most coordinated sauté kid I have ever come across during my long restaurant career. He was the embodiment of grace, speed, and timing. He moved his slender body with the beauty of a dancer. His hands gripped the skillets with dexterity, tossing the ingredients in the air with a precision and gusto that made me smile even on a rotten day. And he didn't toss ingredients together in a skillet at random like some cooks I had seen. He cooked incrementally, one item at a time from scratch. And he was always on top of things, even on weekends when we did close to three hundred covers per night.

I told Alfredo to take over coordinating the orders and support Mario. I reached for the receiver on the other side of the firewall. "Hi, Mike." I sat down on a stool by the pasta cooker, took off my hat, and toyed with it. A cool, soothing breeze blew from the ceiling vent. My feet ached. My face was flushed from the heat of the fifteen-burner stove. And talking to the boss was the last thing I wanted to do because if I lost the flow it would be a bitch catching up. But I didn't have any other choice. I wondered what he wanted. When the boss calls, something is up. And regardless of your skills or title, your heart always trembles a little in anticipation. That's how I felt.

"Just wanted to congratulate you on the good job you are doing." His deep voice resonated from the other end of the line. I switched the phone to my other ear. I was speechless. I didn't know how to accept praise, except to blush. I never got any praise growing up, but it was beautiful to hear those words. I savored each one like a sweet plum. A wave of pride surged in me. In less than a month I had proven myself worthy. I dabbed my moist face with the towel I wore around my neck.

Mike broke in my long silence. "Welcome aboard. That's all I wanted to tell you." "Thank you, Mike," was all I managed to say, a lump of emotion rising in my throat.

"Now get back and keep an eye on the boys. And crank up those numbers. We've got a lot of bills to pay come Monday morning."

That was true. He had built an empire: a string of restaurants and pasta shops all over the South Bay and as far north as Sacramento.

I had landed this job in Silicon Valley just three weeks earlier. Paulo Furiosi, the executive chef of the company, offered it to me after two solid interviews. Trained in classical French cuisine, Paulo, who was born of *Marchigiani* parents, had shifted almost exclusively to Italian cuisine, which at that time was sweeping the country and Europe.

"You have to keep in mind that unlike Europeans, Americans like more ingredients to add texture to their food," Paulo had said, inspecting the dishes he had asked me to prepare at my second interview.

"Take this veal scaloppine you made, for instance." He picked up the plate and examined it with a critic's eye. He brushed the plate with his fat middle finger, and licked the sauce with the grace of a cat. "It's fine in terms of flavor and presentation, and most importantly, the veal isn't overcooked. And by the way, relax: you got the job. I can see you know what you are doing."

I sighed with relief.

"But to an American diner," he continued, "it looks as barren as the Arizona desert. Dress it with mushrooms, tomato *cuncassè*, scallions, and you'll have a dish targeted more to American tastes."

Doubt percolated inside me. Did I have to learn to cook all over again, or was I being awakened to a more marketable approach?

The restaurant, located off De Anza Boulevard, was simply decorated with red-checkered tablecloths. It featured a menu of pasta made on the premises, veal, chicken, pizza, and grilled steaks served with a succulent French sauce of shallots and mushrooms in a red wine reduction finished with a dash of cream and butter. Among the chef's most innovative dishes was seafood cannelloni wrapped in crèpes and baked in a béchamel sauce. However, I thought the food in general lacked Italian authenticity, and when I brought this to Paulo's attention he gave me free rein to improve upon whatever benefited the establishment, as long I didn't stray from the menu. Thus, the daily specials became my experimental lab for my future restaurant.

I located an old Sicilian man who made fresh ricotta and mozzarella cheeses in Walnut Creek—I think he was the only one doing this in northern California at that time—and I introduced mozzarella *caprese*, then polenta, risotto, and *ossi buchi*. The response was immediate and positive. Then I began experimenting with my own recipes and sauces. I was amazed by the results. If they worked here, I thought, why not in Fresno?

Before long I discovered that the corporate world wasn't for me. It was too political and restrictive, with its endless and sometimes fruitless meetings. I don't mind teamwork, but I prefer to steer my own course.

My desire to open my own restaurant was as strong as ever, and the San Joaquin Valley, no matter where I went, still drew me. Perhaps it was its vastness I still marvel at: the endless fields of young grain bending low under the crisp early May wind, or the rich, sweet aroma of must that floated from the wineries in September. And I now had plenty of recipes that had already proved successful. What more could I ask for?

Every week during my day off, I drove to Fresno to see my parents, who had moved to America in the mid-eighties, and to scout the area for a restaurant. I wanted nothing big or extravagant—just a small place with low overhead where I could do most of the work myself. I knew I wouldn't be able to hire employees until the business got rolling.

In 1991, soon after Paulo left the company, I quit and returned to Fresno. It wasn't long before I made a discovery that would transform my life.

SALSA ALLA FRANCESE

SAUCE FRENCH STYLE

Serves 2-4

This sauce is perfect over grilled beef and pork, even chicken breast.

1 tablespoon olive oil	*½ tablespoon minced garlic*
1 tablespoon of unsalted butter	*½ liter good quality red wine*
14-16 oz sliced crimini or regular mushrooms. (I prefer crimini.)	*1 oz unsalted butter*
	2 oz cream
Salt and pepper to taste	*2 tablespoons flat-leaf minced parsley*

In a medium skillet, heat oil and butter over medium heat. Add mushrooms, salt lightly, and cook for a minute. Add garlic. Deglaze with wine and let it reduce by half, about 5-6 minutes. Add cream and let it incorporate a minute or so, or until sauce has reached a medium-thick consistency. Taste for salt and pepper. Add butter and parsley. Spoon over meat.

FOURTEEN

On a warm June day, driving around Fresno, I noticed a thin wisp of smoke crawling out from under the hood of my Corolla. Alarmed by the sight, I pulled into a small strip mall and parked. As I lifted the hood, hot steam spewed everywhere. I stepped back and sat on a waist-high brick wall, folded my arms and waited for the violent rumbling hiss to come to a stop. The bricks under my buttocks felt cool. My eyes fell on the shopping center. It was an ugly, naked, rectangular building of a dozen shops. One caught my attention. On the window of a delicatessen hung a sign that read, "Moving to our new location soon." Perhaps they would be leaving some kitchen fixtures behind. Could this be what I'd been looking for? A small place where I could do volume, yet keep overheads low—from my business experience, this would be the only way I could afford to go into business on my own, considering my meager budget.

This was also the way most old-timers I'd known had done it. Some of them even borrowed money from their parents to put inside the till for change on opening day. These daring men and women, who sometimes barely spoke English, were my unsung American heroes. I salute each and every one of them, wherever they may be, for getting up at the crack of dawn and toiling in kitchens throughout the country to make their customer's dining experience a pleasant one. For their long hours on their feet, their never-ending labor of love, my heart goes out to them.

I slid down from the wall and walked over. When I peered in the window I could hardly see due to the glare of the sun on the glass. I debated what to do. Interrupting a cook during lunch or dinner is blasphemous. But when I glanced at my watch, I realized lunch must be over. It was almost two o'clock. I pushed the door open and stepped inside. A little bell hanging from a hook on the door chimed as I entered. Its jingling sound reminded me of the ones I'd tied around the necks of my goats. A young, spunky blonde behind the counter asked how she could help me. I told her I wanted to speak to the owner. She enquired as to the nature of my request. I said it was personal. She asked my name, and when I told her, she disappeared through a door.

The deli was a long, narrow space. Two bulky white refrigerated display cases sat next to each other. I stood regarding the cold cuts inside the case—bowls of potato salads, macaroni and cheese, olives, links of sausages—wondering whether the life I had led in Italy had really existed. The rich aromas of cold cuts and barbecued meat, and the pungent smell of mustard scented the air. A wooden bench ran along the length of a wall, with six small, round tables with straight-backed wooden chairs lined up against it. The square burgundy vinyl floor was worn, and in several places chipped and badly cracked.

A thick voice broke into my thoughts. "May I help you?" A tall, husky man with thin strands of silver hair stood by the door, drying his hands on a towel.

I introduced myself, explained the purpose of my visit, and pointed to the sign on the window. The man's pale blue eyes fell on me searchingly, a reaction I discovered people with foreign accents often receive in this country.

"Come on back," he finally said, "but don't look at the mess."

"Don't worry, I'm used to the business," I offered.

I followed the man through the kitchen door. It was the smallest kitchen I'd ever laid eyes on—no more than fifteen feet long by ten wide. A six-foot galvanized hood hung from a wall above a four-burner stove. Great. A hood would be the biggest expense, especially if I had to buy it and have it installed. If he planned to leave it, I'd save several thousand dollars. Next to it sat a three-compartment stainless steel sink. I could see no dishwasher anywhere, and worse, no place to put one. In the back, sacks of briquettes were piled in a heap on the floor. Dirty chafing dishes were on the floor and a load of delivery boxes had been stacked high by the back door. Plenty of merchandise stocked on the overhead wood shelves indicated he was doing good business. My brain spun trying to visualize how I could rearrange it.

"What will you leave behind?" I asked, envisioning the business potential. The line of prospective customers like in

Silicon Valley. Or the dread of silent waiting, hoping to fill the tables every night. Which would it be? Would I be able to generate sufficient volume to cover expenses and show a profit? Or should I keep looking instead of listening to my gut instinct, which was strong? As strong as it had ever been. A little voice whispered in my head. *This is it. Take it. Don't let it slip you by, even if you think it isn't perfect.*

"The sink, the hood, and this walk-in refrigerator," the man said, slapping the wall against which he was leaning. This news seemed too good to be true. Inside I shook with excitement. I tried to hide it to leverage the deal. During the last couple of years I'd seen innumerable establishments, but none that affected me the way this place did. I'd been searching for perfection, but it had only existed in my head. Until now. And now I knew that this was the one. There was equipment in place, plenty of parking, and the location was excellent. And location was everything. It was a go, if the price was right. Forget the price. How much could he ask for this old equipment? It would cost him more to rip it out. It would be a go. For lunch and take out I could manage without a dishwasher. I'd serve on paper plates if I had to.

After a short, easy round of negotiations, I wrote him a check for the deposit, on the condition that the landlord would give me a new lease. Without prior business experience I feared I might yet be turned down. He told me to relax because the landlord was a reasonable man. We sealed the deal with a solid handshake.

I walked out, put water in the radiator while the sun warmed my back, and drove home. I still had to go to my cooking job in Hanford, and I'd so lost track of time. I hadn't called Mama to tell her I was running late. She'd be worried.

I pulled up to the curb under the Modesto Ash tree in front of the house and parked. I sat there a moment listening to the *ting ting ting* of the engine cooling off. It was an older but well kept neighborhood, with fairly well kept front yards and mature trees flanking the street. The homes weren't luxurious by any means, but modest and cozy, simple in design—like most homes in America—offering easy access through the drive to the garage. This quality was so advantageous for loading and unloading, and so uniquely American, that my parents revered it as perhaps the best and most convenient feature of the entire house.

John across the street was a sweet but intimidating-looking fellow. I was glad he looked out for my parents, though disappointed he couldn't communicate with them except by hand-waving. But I knew John would happily watch out for them as long as they always sent him scampering home with a bottle of my father's homemade wine under his log-thick arm.

The house was a single story with fading yellow walls and gray plastic shingles. It wasn't nearly as elegant as our apartment in Milano. Mama complained about the old-fashioned window with a lever and the gray carpet. "The dirt hides in it," she lamented, preferring tiles instead. She had planted rose bushes along the front wall. They bloomed in a mosaic of colors now.

My father had turned the ample yard into a garden. In it he grew tomatoes, fava beans, sweet peppers, eggplant, sage, rosemary, basil, and other seasonal vegetables.

I'd bought them a satellite setup when these first became available. Pointing southeast from the rooftop, it received an Italian channel, RAI, that played a host of programs, including many political talk shows, Mama's favorites. My reasoning behind it was simple: it kept my parents connected to the old world. In a town where they didn't drive, had no extended family, there wasn't an Italian community per se, and they didn't understand the language, this was the only tie to their world. I couldn't fathom what it would be like living like that.

My parents never went anywhere, except grocery shopping. Father pushed the market's cart down the sidewalk, and Mama trudged behind him, her worn brown purse dangling from her wrist, while neighbors watched amused at the weekly ritual parading before their eyes. New leaves sprouted, turned yellow, and floated to the ground.

My parents never expected to go anywhere. They'd retained that simple lifestyle of Southern Italy which revolves around family. An occasional lunch or dinner out to Teppanyak to celebrate Mother's Day or Father's Day, would suffice for them for months. Besides, with what it cost to eat out, Mama could have shopped for a week, put food on the table for days, saved considerable money at the end of the year, she used to say. And when I convinced her to come, she'd choose the least expensive items on the menu. It was difficult for Mama to indulge in such luxuries. Eating out was something she couldn't conceive of, something only the rich could afford, something well beyond her means, she believed. On the other hand, Father had no problem going out to eat. He was more adventuresome, would eat just about anything that was brought to him, and didn't worry about price.

Frequently we had a lot of close friends and acquaintances over. The gatherings were intimate, with people my parents knew and felt comfortable with, Americans and Italians. This, above all forms of entertainment, my parents enjoyed most.

When I stepped from the car, the rich aroma of fried onions and tomato sauce tickled my senses. Mama had cooked something good again.

Inside, in the kitchen, I told her about the transaction, and she got upset that I'd made the deal without first consulting her. "I don't count for anything in this house." Her words rang with anger and disappointment. "I'm only a slave here. That's what I am. Two men in the house to cook and wash for when I can barely take care of myself, with all my aches and pains. "Her chest heaved and shook with emotions, her face flushed. Mama drew a deep breath, then barreled on like an unstoppable train. "Because I'm stupid. That's why. Stupid! Should paint my nails, sit around drink coffee and smoke, cook two or three times a week, and take clothes to the dry cleaners like some women in this neighborhood do. That's what I should do, and not be a servant." She stopped to catch her breath, and then dashed on again. "Swear one of these days I'm packing up and moving back to Calabria where I belong. Leave you alone like dogs, I will. Humpf! Maybe then somebody will appreciate me. Besides, don't want to die in a foreign land. No, *Signore mio*." She raised her hands to heaven and rotated about the kitchen in a frenzy, seemingly propelled by the winds of her own desperation. Her lips were trembling like a child about to cry.

My stomach churned with misery. All the fibers of my nerve endings tingled and rustled like dry grass blown by the wind.

This last remark was a heavy burden to live with. I wanted to get up and leave, tell her to stop this nonsense. Because death was death no matter where it occurred. "I want to die in my village where I was born," she insisted every time the subject came up. This, to her, was serious business. I wanted to scream *mea culpa* for having uprooted them now. I bit my tongue. But it frightened her to die in a foreign land, far from her birthplace. Perhaps deep within her—deep in every countryman there is a longing to come full circle at the end, to return to one's starting point. Just like the salmon who migrate upstream to their place of origin, immigrants seem driven by the instinct to return home, to their final resting place.

Although Mama lived in the past like many Italians, to her credit, she had been trying to adjust to America. But after nearly a decade in Fresno she was still adjusting. She often lamented that the town lacked a unified Italian community where people could congregate like they did in the piazzas in Italy and get out of the house for awhile to be with other humans. The saddest thing Mama had discovered about rural America was that hardly anyone walked the streets after dusk.

Mama had never been too keen to come to America, even if she had expressed the desire to Al, probably out of desperation to get out of Nonna's house. She longed to be close to her aunt Mary in California, but the idea of leaving Italy frightened her. Aunt Mary was her deceased father's younger sister. They had been corresponding for years, and slowly, Mama began to nurture a special affection and bond toward her aunt.

Aunt Mary, who included a crumpled dollar bill or two in her letters and sent an occasional package of clothes for Christmas, empathized with the tragedy my mother incurred by losing her father when she was only a few years old—a loss Mama never got over.

One might speculate that Al's arrival was fate brewing its own concoctions of future events. And if it hadn't been for Aunt Mary, Al would never have showed up on Nonna's doorstep, and I might never have come to America. Looking back, my life seems interwoven like a spider web. At one end of the spectrum stands Aunt Mary, on the other, my grandfather. These two forces merged on that cold April day when Al arrived, swept me off my feet, and hurled me across the Atlantic, so to speak. And once my two brothers joined me in California, there was no more reason for my parents to stay back in the old country. To an Italian mother of that generation, it was unthinkable to live separated from her children. In fact, her whole life revolved around them.

Over time, Mama had come to realize that being an immigrant meant living each day in an unsettled state of mind, a sort of suspended existence created by continuous reminders of who you once were. The way of life that once defined you was gone now. And what heightened this turmoil was the dim hope that someday you would return to your homeland. This left you psychologically straddling two continents.

But her keen eye noticed the beauty and efficiency of America as well. My parents both marveled that everyone at the post office drew numbers and stood civilly in line waiting their turn. They were shocked that you were allowed to pick and choose your own produce at the grocery counter. They were amazed at the friendliness and courtesy with which American merchants treated customers, and blown away by the fact that you could return a pair of shoes that hadn't made you happy, and, incredibly, get your money back. Only in America was this possible.

Mama's words still stung, and a strong urge to get up and leave seized me again. How could anyone blame her? I was late and hadn't called her, and the fact that the food had gone cold only added insult to injury.

"So you decided you are going to take on such an endeavor after all, uhm?" Mama cut in after a long silence, bent over the stove, her eyes drifting to me, her spiteful spirit piercing me like a lance. "And just how are you going to run a business all by yourself? Without employees? Your father and I think you are gambling big time." She laid the wooden spoon across the ridge of the pan and stepped closer to me. "But I'm not going to say another word on the subject. *Basta*. I have said all there is to be said. Besides, my words always fall on deaf ears. Do as you wish. I hope you know that you won't have health insurance now, unless you pay for it out of your own pocket. How do you like that? Hahaa." She paused and glared at me with disappointment, even a hint of disdain, panting as if she had run up a flight of stairs. She leaned forward, inches from my face, looked deep into my eyes. "What did you go to school for, all those years, eh? To open a restaurant?" I could feel her warm breath. I felt lousy. My lips were dry. Mama's face was mottled with sad disappointment. She concluded her litany of complaints, held up her hand to signal that the conversation was over, and the door on the subject shut. I was about to say something, utter some apology to her retreating back. But it wouldn't have made any difference. When she got like this, she became impenetrable.

The truth always hurts. No matter who the bearer is.

I had indulged in languages, studied sciences, immersed myself in the humanities, searched for the meaning of life in philosophy throughout my university years, and now here I was about ready to open a restaurant. It didn't make any sense to me either. I had spent thousands of my hard earned dollars in foreign tuition over time, more than Mama even knew, unlike many fellow students whose parents paid for everything. I had basked in all that knowledge that now seemed utterly useless to run a restaurant, as it was turning out. But at least it didn't bother me as much as it did Mama. I suppose she still couldn't understand that I'd never had to conform to traditional expectations. I thought of Emerson's "self reliance" and for a moment it helped me to plow through Mama's resistance, lifting my wounded spirit. Nonetheless, among the few disadvantages of being the oldest sibling in an Italian family—carrying the psychological burden of the entire family on my shoulder like a stigmata— there was one great consolation. I got my way most of the time. And this occasion was no exception. Although I have no way of knowing this, I presume that every nationality carries its burden, handed down from generation to generation. Whether for good or bad, it's another matter. But this was my own.

I observed Mama in her element: the kitchen. The counter was cluttered with jars of dried herbs. Two basil plants on the windowsill would bask in the winter sun until she sacrificed them leaf by leaf in her cooking. She hovered over her four-burner gas stove, the center of her domain, with care and a little cockiness, like a proud mother hen. To say she was territorial would be an understatement. She might as well have posted a No Trespassing sign.

It was hard for me sit idly and watch another person cook, even Mama. My attention was drawn to that little imperfection, that tiny wasted movement, that one awkward procedure that complicated work instead of simplifying it.

But I let myself enjoy the scene unfolding before my eyes because I didn't dare to tell her anything. And regardless of my perceptions, there's no denying the glow of pleasure that sparkled in Mama's eyes when she cooked, happy, undisturbed, and unhurried. It made no difference whether she was mincing parsley, grating Parmigiano with her ancient grater, or scooping up a plate of pasta for her beloved grandson or daughter-in-law.

These were the simple pleasures that gave meaning to her daily life.

I reached for the phone and called the deli owner, telling him I had to show the place to my business partner. I translated for her. She brushed me away like a fly, then turned on the gas stove, picked up her burned wooden spoon, and stabbed at the food in the pan with no handles—she had two, which I didn't dare to throw away. What was she making with such violence? Polenta? I didn't think so. She scooped the semblance of an eggplant *parmigiana* onto a plate, threw a few strands of spaghetti on the side, poured a spoonful of tomato sauce on it, and brought it to the table. Her breath whistled through her nose as she plunked it down, lips primly pursed. "*Ecco, vostra altezza è servito.*" Here, your highness is served. My appetite was long gone, but I was going to eat it for fear she might pick up the plate and hurl it out the window.

MELENZANE ALLA PARMIGIANA

EGGPLANT PARMESAN

2 large eggplant

¾ cup grated Parmigiano

3 cups vegetable oil for frying

4-5 whole fresh mozzarella, sliced

14-16 oz marinara sauce

salt to taste

Rinse and dry eggplant. Cut off tops and ends and discard. Leave skin on. Cut lengthwise into ¼ inch slices. Lay slices on a long dish or baking pan and sprinkle with salt. The salt will release the bitter eggplant juice. Let rest for about 30 minutes. Pat dry sweat from slices with paper towels.

Pour oil into a medium-size skillet over medium heat and let it get very hot. Cautiously lower each slice into hot oil. Cook until they are golden on both sides, about 2 minutes. Remove and place on paper towel to drain. Repeat process until finished. Sprinkle cooked slices lightly with salt.

Preheat oven to 350.

Cover the bottom of a baking dish with a ladle of marinara sauce. Let your personal preference be your guide here. Follow with a layer of eggplant slices overlapping each other by a few inches. Spread more sauce over eggplant. Sprinkle with Parmigiano, mozzarella slices or cubes, scattered chopped basil leaves. Repeat process twice more. Place dish into oven and cook for about 15-20 minutes. Let it set a couple of minutes, then serve.

FIFTEEN

Fresno, California, 1991

Discouraged by the grand fiasco of our first day in business, I forged ahead with a menu comprised of seventy-five percent pasta dishes. I also offered a good selection of sandwiches, the beloved pasta salads, and my free in-house marketing research: the daily specials. In a few weeks, just as I'd anticipated, it became clear to me that in order to stay in business I'd have to tap into the evening trade. There wasn't enough money to sustain me with lunch and take-out alone.

Uncertainty can send my mind skidding down the dark alley of depression when I can't solve a problem. Although I may be daring at times, give me uncertainty for too long and my values become questionable and my self-confidence sinks. I have no clue how other men think, but for me these two qualities make up that delicate and intricate pattern that supports my entire internal structure like the walls of a house. But what else was there for me to do except wait it out and not lose hope? Sometimes this is the only thing a man has left. It can make the difference between life and death, sanity and insanity, defeat and victory. I'd no idea what lay ahead.

What obstacles might be in my way. Or what my best course of action would be. This endeavor was turning out to be as enigmatic as the trip to America. But I knew that the answer, whatever it was, lay at the end of the journey. For there would be no other way to know.

Despite this setback, I wasn't going to surrender, allow defeat to enter the equation. I kept listening diligently to my motivational tapes in the crackling player of my Corolla. One tape in particular filled me with goose bumps, hope, and determination—sometimes tears, too. It referred to a boy who had been born a hunchback. Determined to overcome his handicap at all costs, every day the boy stretched his back further and further, one inch at a time, until he stood straight and erect like the statue in the distance he had modeled himself after. Some days, this image alone sustained me.

I'd keep going with the same setup I used at lunch: serve dinner on paper plates, with plastic cups and flatware. If I was lucky enough to make it through the first year, I might be all right. True, some people were going to ridicule me for this bold move, and probably assume I was an amateur cook as well. Possibly a nut. In my head, I could hear the town's collective criticism playing a mocking chorus. But there was no turning back.

To survive in this ruthless industry, quality and value would become my weapons. The restaurant was simple and clean, reflecting my personal philosophy about food and life. Forget the white linen tablecloths, the sparkling wine glasses, and the fancy setups I'd been used to all along. Deep inside

I wanted to cry, to purge myself of the mortal sin of serving pasta on paper plates. One thing was for sure: my reputation and career would begin here, or end.

My only decorations were the long strands of fresh pasta hanging from wooden rods along one wall and above the show-window and several framed prints of old Milano. When you stood by the door and peered inside, it was quaint, like the *trattorie* in Italy. Then, as you entered, the rich aromas of baking *focaccia*, rosemary, garlic, and olive oil would pull you deeper inside. I even contemplated rerouting the aromas emanating from the exhaust hood on the rooftop toward the front of the building to attract customers: *If they smell it, they will come.* But I could never figure out how to lay an inconspicuous pipeline.

With a new menu in hand, I extended the hours until nine in the evening, seven days a week. Most nights, by the time Mama and I cleaned the stove and kitchen and swept and mopped the floor, it was close to midnight. The old job with its gossip and politics didn't seem so bad now. I hadn't put in seventeen-hour days, much less done janitorial work, for years.

Days came and went as I stood before the stove with my aching feet and sore back while the valley's sweltering heat seeped in through the ceiling and exuded through the pores of my skin. What had once been my shoes were now blobs of oil, tomato sauce, and flour.

I couldn't have managed without Mama's help. Although she had no clue how a restaurant kitchen was operated, years of cooking at home had provided her with a good apprenticeship. Moreover, she was an inspired cook. A couple of potatoes, a few mixed vegetables, shells or corkscrew-shaped pasta, a generous drizzle of olive oil, and in no time she would have a meal ready. Or a light *minestra* concocted with whatever greens were available from the garden. Her peasant approach to food was stunning, humbling.

About seventy-five percent of restaurant work is preparation, a labor-intensive process even for an experienced prep-person. Mama was overwhelmed by the fast pace of working the line, the system of preparation I had in place, and the infinite variety of ingredients necessary to compose each dish. Mama seemed a little lost, as though her mind couldn't justify all those ingredients. But there was a new and subtle reticence to her demeanor—she knew that this was my domain and she couldn't prevail nor boss me around. As a child, my world was colored and filtered through her eyes. But now that role had been reversed.

I tried to show Mama the professional way of using a knife for speedy chopping. "*Cosi,*" I said, going through the motions.

She tilted her head sideways. Beneath her carved-stone cheekbones and her small, graceful mouth, a malicious smile quivered. I could see a little hostility growing in her. She shifted her weight from one foot to the other, folded her arms, and surveyed me with a twinkle of challenge in her warm eyes—Mama's eyes had different levels. Now they were looking through me. My eyes peeled away from hers, landed inside the deli-case, and glided over the flat wicker baskets containing fresh pasta packaged in clear plastic bags. I could feel a roaring laughter rising inside my chest like distant thunder, but I stifled it. "You think you know it all, don't you?" she remarked, bridging the gap between us with a confrontational stride. "Just because you went to college you think the rest of us have no brains." She wagged a finger in my face. "But let me remind you just for the record that you don't." A stab of guilt rippled through me. I should have known that telling my mother how to hold a knife would hurt her feelings.

I observed her struggling with the new technique for a while, wondering who this woman really was that I called mother, who loved me unconditionally, with no ulterior motives. Who resided inside that body? Then I told her to go back to her own way lest she chop off a finger. She cast me a diffident glance and picked up her pace again. She was slow, but steady, and I guess that's what mattered. She plowed through at her own speed, producing mounds of chopped scallions, sliced mushrooms, and diced tomato, sometimes for hours on end.

I watched the gentle sway of her shoulders as she leaned over the wooden table, watched her arthritic knuckles chop away steadily. These were the same hands untouched by manicures or nail polish—ever—that had wiped my nose, tucked me into bed, and patched my trousers and socks for years on end. Meaty, but well defined, there was a gracefulness running down the length of each finger like a sort of sculpture. The palms were creased and tough, denoting her perennial love for the soil, pulling weeds and planting. These were hands so dear I wanted to hold and kiss them to express my gratitude for all they had done for me. Mama had been making the best of all situations all of her life, and it was no different now. Her loving, golden hands were still helping me. I treasured these moments, the pleasant and the unpleasant, aware that one day Mama would be gone. Then I would remember these hours spent with her as gifts of love frozen in time.

I looked at my own hands. They were scraped and bruised from opening and dismantling cardboard boxes, painful from years of handling skillets. My wrists ached when the weather changed. On my right forefinger there was an oil blister, a red, watery pustule that bubbled and throbbed, which hindered my ability to work comfortably, slowed me down. Little injuries like this made me realize the fragility of the body, that I took health for granted. "Poor working hands," I thought aloud. Mama turned around with enquiring eyes. She was like a radar—nothing escaped her.

With almost forty entrées the menu was too vast for such a small kitchen. The six-burner stove in reality had only four burners. Two burners were always taken by pots for boiling pasta. Nonetheless, I was determined to offer dishes loaded with flavors and texture. The food had to be wholesome, simple, soulful, like the cuisine of my own country, and made with the best ingredients available. I don't know of too many cuisines where you can whip up a healthy meal, sometimes in minutes, using simple ingredients. In France, we prepared dishes with flour, eggs, butter, and cream. Mussels drowned in white wine and cream sauce, for example. Italian cuisine marries unrivaled variety with simplicity of execution—most times—and unpretentious elegance in presentation. Although I respect French cuisine, and I'm fond of many of its classical dishes like the *côte de boeuf* and *daube* of beef Provençal, I still prefer Italian cooking. And I can't think of any culture in Europe that can rival Italians when it comes to our endless variety of appetizers. Only the Spanish come close.

I figured if there were enough people in town that liked my homey style of cooking, I'd have to succeed. Particularly if I offered service as well—a quality which every single business should thrive on, but alas, is often badly lacking. There is no excuse for failing at this. It doesn't require an extra investment in capital. Only attitude, knowledge, and kind words directed at prospective customers' desires, wants, and needs. This is what customer service is all about. And unlike flavor, which is usually, but not always, commensurate with the cook's experience, service is a free commodity. Sometimes, it alone can keep a business afloat.

Moreover, I also offered a choice of several dishes prepared according to the guidelines of the American Heart Association, to separate myself from the competition and to satisfy my passion for healthy eating. In these instances, I used only a teaspoon of unheated oil to flavor the dish. It was during these moments that I remembered Nonna reusing frying oil several times to economize. I chuckled at the memory.

Food value had to be paramount. Consumers seem to be hardwired with an internal alarm that alerts them when a product isn't priced fairly, food or otherwise. I don't know how, but they just know. They may be taken once, twice, three times at the most, but never again. Whose loss is it? The business'. For the consumer has a million other choices. These two elements, quality and value, I'd no doubt, would give me the edge over the competition. I structured the menu and specials based on this formula. A formula I'd repeatedly seen defeat competition and bad economic times over the years.

Daily specials usually reflect the personal preferences of the cook. Here I indulged my creativity and took advantage of local seasonal items, which were varied and plentiful in our rich valley. Doing so helps support the community, especially those few people that take pride in what they do. You can soon spot them because they shine like gold in a world of mediocrity. That's how it ought to be. Buy locally, and don't fatten the impersonal corporate structure of commercial food manufacturers. I often wondered where the produce, meat, poultry or fish supplied by the major wholesalers had been manufactured.

Dinner was slow: two or three tables per night—four when we were lucky. I cooked with a clear view of the narrow dining area. It looked like the dining car of a train. Mama helped slice bread for customers, set placemats on the naked tables, bussed, fetched items I needed for a particular dish, washed and dried skillets by hand, and helped me carry plates to the table. Frequently, I poured either wine or liquor into a skillet, which caused a tongue of fire to leap two or three feet into the air. It was a spectacle children relished with amused eyes, and invariably mentioned to their parents. "Wow, did you see what the cook just did?" Mama moaned in passing that I was a braggart, because in the end, none of that showy stuff added any flavor to the food.

Nonetheless, she always greeted customers with a profound appreciation. "Halloooo," she would say, menus in hand, eyes glistening with pleasure at whoever stumbled in.

One evening it was so slow that I decided to close early. Mama was putting chairs upside-down on the tables and I was in the back gulping down polenta with a cold beer while cleaning the stove, when a soothing woman's voice trailed into the kitchen. What seemed strange was that the familiar voice spoke a few words of Italian, trying to communicate with Mama. "*Ciao, Maria*," the lovely voice said. This caught my fancy. I turned around and couldn't believe my eyes. It was Jane. My heart danced pirouettes. A wave of dizziness swept over me. Was I dreaming?

"*Ciao*," Jane called, still holding Mama's hand in an affectionate gesture. Her eyes met mine for a fleeting moment. I felt a weakness in my knees, a pounding inside my chest. I forced a feeble smile as her presence reignited old emotions. Fifteen years had gone by since the day she had left Milano's train station in a frenzy. Yet she had hardly changed. A few more pounds padded the slender lining of her body. I had run into her once in town after she got married, and then an awkward smile, an uncomfortable glance, and a whisper of good-bye were all we had exchanged. I wondered about the nature of this unexpected visit. "Well, well, look who is here," I said, sounding fake as can be. I wiped my hands on the towel hanging from the belt of my apron, and walked to her. I'm sure Mama took in every nuance of our reunion.

I lifted four chairs down from a table, and we sat. Soon, unable to follow the conversation, Mama excused herself and hobbled to the kitchen.

"Care for a glass of wine?" I asked.

She chose beer instead. I got a Moretti out of the fridge, uncapped it, and brought it to her.

"So, how is business?" she asked, her eyes roaming the place, her head bobbing as though she approved of the decor. Her sun-bleached hair had lost a little of its luster. I looked at her, fighting a deep longing to wrap my arms around her, caress her flushed cheeks.

"To be honest, it could be better. Much better," I confessed.

"Well, it's gonna take some time. But you will be fine. People are talking about you in town."

"They are?" I was surprised to hear this news. But Fresno was still a tight-knit community, a quaint town where tongues flapped and news traveled fast. Particularly news about a new restaurant. It seemed as though the whole town flocked to newly opened restaurants like the faithful on a pilgrimage. Though not in my case. I wondered why.

Jane's hand clasped the bottle. She nodded.

I could see Mama casting furtive glances from the kitchen. I wondered what was going through her head. "I hope it's good," I said.

"It is. Trust me," she said, bringing the bottle to her lips and taking a satisfying sip, her warm eyes gazing into mine. The bottle was beaded with moisture. "Just don't let it get to your head." She grinned. Old Jane.

But was I really going to be all right? Although I admired America's perennial optimism, I'd inherited my parent's gloom and doom mentality.

"*Fur you*," Mama said, approaching the table with a plate of appetizers she'd prepared herself. Prosciutto, wedges of Parmigiano, sun-dried tomatoes, olives, and a basket of focaccia. She sat them in front of Jane and flashed a big smile.

"Oh, my God," said Jane, blushing. She looked up at Mama and squeezed her hand.

Mama thrust her head back, and her eyes grew proud.

"*Eet, eet*," Mama said, patting Jane's shoulder. She walked back to the kitchen.

"I just ate." Jane stared at me.

I smiled. "You don't want to hurt her feelings, do you?"

We engaged in ritual talk. Slowly, Jane cleaned her plate. I couldn't believe this was happening. I remembered the arguments and cultural differences we had shared in Milano. Somehow, I'd seen her in a different light after she got to Italy.

She'd put up a good front to please me, struggling to adjust to a culture that was as remote to her as night to day. And the facts that she smoked, and wore jeans and not a skirt, were nearly scandalous to my relatives. "What's the matter? Why don't you tell her to wear a nice skirt? Beautiful girl like that, it's shame to wear pants," Nonna had whispered into my ear the minute after I introduced Jane to the family. Her Anglo-Saxon looks and her casual dress turned a lot of heads when we walked down the sidewalk. At one point I'd entertained the idea of taking her to Calabria to show her where I was born. But I soon gave it up, certain I'd be excommunicated by my relatives. If Jane complained Milano was a macho man's world, I didn't dare to imagine what she'd think of feudal Calabria. No wonder we hadn't lasted. But now none of that seemed important, what mattered was to seize the thrill of the moment, bask in the glow of her presence.

The metal mop-bucket squeaked as Mama rolled it along the floor. It had been a long day. Mama's face was drawn and she moved as if her feet ached. Jane pushed back her chair and stood up. "Well, time for me to head home and make sure my kids haven't set the house on fire."

I told her she hadn't lost her sense of humor. She said that was about all she had left. She kissed Mama on the cheeks, and then embraced her. Mama held her tight. "*Arrivederci*," said Jane, raising her arm and smiling at Mama as I walked her out.

Mama waved, returning the smile. I remembered when Jane had left the Milano train station. Mama had gone through the same motions as the train rolled away, except that a few tears had coursed down her cheeks. I promised myself then that I'd never cause my mother any more such pain. I'd keep any future relationship secret from her until I was sure. She didn't deserve extra burdens piled on her. Life had granted her plenty of hardships.

In the kitchen Mama said, "We should take him something to eat before we go," pointing outside toward the homeless man lying in the semidarkness.

"No, we shouldn't." We'd been feeding him often. But a few days earlier he'd barked a string of wild obscenities when I took him a plate of pasta. And I had no idea why. Maybe he felt humiliated. You can never tell about people. "If he is that hungry, he can always knock on the door. We'll feed him." I could feel the terseness in my words. I knew Mama felt it too. I didn't like it. But I wasn't going to take a chance.

As I drove out of the center, night was falling on the town. Lights glowed inside the few open shops. Api, the shoemaker, was still hammering away behind his counter. Jack and Dawn, the jewelers, had long closed shop and gone home for the evening. The young service station attendant at the 76 gas station across the street leaned over one of the pumps and stared into space, bored stiff. Under the dome of the hazy sky, the night was descending quietly over Fresno.

On the way home neither Mama nor I said a word. I drove down Bullard Avenue thinking how strange, random, and unpredictable life can be.

"Wasn't…wasn't that nice that she stopped by?" Mama ventured. The Central Valley heat lingered thick and damp like a sodden blanket. It rose from the seams of the boiling earth like misery and hung in the air. The electric sign at Glendale Savings and Loan registered ninety-eight degrees. A cluster of redwood trees along the road stood still and dark against the hazy sky. My head felt empty. I couldn't think of anything, except that business wasn't going well. And now to add to my pressures, Jane had to materialize out of nowhere and stir my old emotions.

"Why didn't you marry her?" Mama blurted out.

Folded in the seat next to me, Mama looked small. But that was just the deceptive glow of the soft evening light falling on the contours of her face. For under that rumpled mint-green dress she wore, the bag of skin and arthritic bones, there was a rock of a woman.

Marry her? Where was this coming from? "Excuse me?" I turned my head sideways.

"What are you glaring at? Can't you see you are getting old and you haven't got a family? Before you know it you will become like a wilted *cavolo*: an old cauliflower."

I wished she wouldn't compare me with a vegetable. I wasn't one by a long shot. Of course I knew everything she'd said. I didn't need her to remind me. She'd always hoped I'd marry an Italian woman. It would have made things so much easier for Mama, particularly the language. She gesticulated her way through a conversation with grunts, nods, and uncertain smiles. Even her daughter-in-law and grandson she couldn't understand. And the little Nonna said rarely made sense to them either.

"Not even a dog should live alone, let alone *una persona*. And who is going to iron your clothes, cook, and look after you when you get old and I'm not around anymore?"

Those words swept through me like an icy storm. The air suddenly became too thick, too heavy to inhale. The thought terrified me now as much as it had when I was a child. I'd gained not an ounce of strength in all these years to face this inevitability. I wanted to scream and pull my hair out. But what infuriated me even more was that all she said was true.

"Angela back home is still available. That sweet girl never married. You know?" Mama kept in touch with the old country by telephone, and by reading *L'italo-Americano* newspaper. This was essential to her, for it kept her past alive.

"I wonder why," I said. "She wasn't exactly a beauty."

A long silence followed. A palpable tension hovered between us. Mama shifted in the seat. I winced.

Here we go.

I knew she was getting revved up to unleash one of her little speeches again.

"You think beauty is everything, don't you. Well, let me tell you: it isn't. It's what's inside here that counts in a person." She tapped her bosom, and gave me an uneasy glance. Mama seemed to always have an answer ready. I speculated it might be the wisdom that comes with aging.

But I couldn't change my nature. "Sorry to disappoint you, Ma, but if I feel no chemistry, I don't know if I could love or marry any woman."

Mama was stumped. She stroked the side of her short wavy gray hair with one hand. "Then, *figlio mio*, you don't know what true love is," she said with raised eyebrows and pursed lips. She crossed her arms and looked out the window at the passing scenery.

Silence.

Mama shifted her gaze, looked at me searchingly, and adopted the manner of little girls when they mimic one another.

"Sorry to disappoint you, but if I feel no *chemistry*—what the hell is the matter with you, uh?" she asked. "You are a grown man. Not a boy anymore. Chemistry, uh? You have *paglia*, hay, up here." She twisted her forefinger against her temple, turned her neck and looked away.

If it were possible to judge the depths of disappointment on her face, I guessed she was well beyond any reconciliation, no matter what I said, or how tactfully I said it.

We drove in silence. Mama slumped back into the seat as if a great weight of sorrow had been thrust upon her shoulders. Her words sent my mind scrambling in search of solutions to problems that had no answers. I pondered about the life I might have left behind on the other side of the Atlantic. And I thought about Mama being in my face every chance she got, just because she loved me and wanted the best for me. Who could blame her? What mother wouldn't want to see her son settled with a devoted wife and a few *bambini*? Where had I gone wrong? I didn't spill any tears, but inside I was crying.

Deep inside me somewhere a panic attack was surging, gaining momentum by the second, like a flood ready to engulf me. I braced myself for the fury that was about to erupt. I told myself this too would pass, like all the others. I took a deep breath. Waited.

"Remember that there will come a time when there won't be any more time," Mama said out of the blue. She seemed like an inexhaustible source of wisdom. And here I was beginning to think of myself as a writer. It occurred to me that Mama had never severed my umbilical cord. I had no children, but speculated a mother's love and concern for the well-being of her child never ends, no matter what his age. Although Mama's devotion to my happiness at times seemed annoying and overbearing, ultimately I was glad she hadn't cut that cord after all.

As I drove home, the rustling summer evening was fading. It was that magic time when day was transitioning into night, conjuring up sweet images of family life, when most worries are put temporarily aside. And thinking of Jane, a tender promise lingered in the air. Over the horizon, the sun had left the sky swathed in red and gold.

Another sweltering day would descend over the valley tomorrow.

POLENTA

Serves 5-6

7 cups water

2 cups of coarse polenta
(Preferably imported. It has
a firmer texture. Or use the
common mush, as it is often
called.)

1 cup milk

2 oz unsalted butter

1 tablespoon salt

In a heavy pot over medium heat, bring water to a boil. Add the milk. Let water reach a boil again. Add salt and butter, and dissolve with whisk. Slowly pour the polenta into the water with one hand and whisk it with the other so that no lumps are formed. Now that the cornmeal has been thoroughly incorporated, use a wooden spoon to stir frequently. Be very careful—as the polenta thickens and bubbles, it will spit back with greater vengeance than boiling water. Continue stirring and dislodging lumps that form around the edges of the pot. The polenta is ready when it peels easily away from the sides, 35 to 40 minutes.

At this stage, polenta is soft and ready to be eaten with a sauce of your choice. To eat it the next day, butter a baking dish, pour the hot polenta into it, rub the surface with butter so it doesn't form a crust, let cool at room temperature. Cover it with plastic wrap and stow in the refrigerator. Polenta can be baked, grilled, broiled, and, of course, reheated and topped with your favorite sauce.

SIXTEEN

It is my nature to ponder things. Sometimes too long, and to the point of obsession, often getting stuck in a rut. I don't know how other minds work, but mine is like a gopher. It digs deep into the dark cavern of the unknown, that vast and sometimes untapped region of the unconscious. Once there, I explore and consider all possibilities to tackle and try to solve a problem. I dig up an answer, or, if I'm unable to, I relinquish the task to the higher wisdom of the mind to come up with one. Usually this last technique yields wonders. And that's what I'd done with the store. I'd borrowed money from a friend to keep my venture going and was beginning to lose sleep over it. How much longer could I keep pumping money into the business? I hadn't imagined that in a small town with little competition it would prove so difficult to generate enough volume to show a profit. I'd had visions of people stampeding into the restaurant. It's funny how easily man rearranges reality in his mind to suit his desires.

I was familiar enough with the trade to know I should have had enough money to carry me at least through the first year of operation. What I was doing now was foolish and disastrous because it is due to lack of sufficient capital that eighty-five percent of new restaurants fail. Opening the business without running capital was like going to war without the proper armor, jumping into the water unable to swim. But circumstances and time had slowly jostled and nudged me along like a twig floating down a river, and brought me to this point. I had to take the plunge now or never. There comes a time in everyone's life when a decision has to be made, a direction taken, and this was my turn to cross the Rubicon. I'd taken a chance, and now I was learning from the real teacher: life.

"Somebody has put a curse on my family. That's why things never work out for us. *Madonna mia, protegici tu*, watch over us." Mama rambled on, making the sign of the cross, and looking up toward heaven. According to her, someone had put the *Malocchio*, the evil eye, on us.

Unable to make the drops of oil into the cup of holy water dissolve into minuscule ripples with her prayers—Mama's ritual to dispel the *Malocchio* from family members, me in this case—she suggested a second anointing. I wasn't sure if it would make any difference. I knew her love for me was such that she would do almost anything in her power to help me succeed. She would have walked on water, if she could, to help me.

But wasn't I supposed to be the leader of this venture? The one with the knowledge to navigate the intricacies of the business world? I chided myself for adding more worries to Mama's life. If I had been successful working for others, why was I stumbling now? And to let Mama come to my rescue seemed demeaning, especially to let her perform a ritual of dubious validity. But I felt helpless. I surrendered to my childish illusion that Mama could still right any wrong that had befallen her little boy. Besides, Mama had a quality I hadn't: faith. I accepted her heartfelt offer.

She said she wanted to go to church this time, light a candle to Saint Anthony and pray. It would be a more efficacious anointing this way, she explained. Saint Anthony had been her patron saint ever since we were in Pezzolo. Every year, in spring, Mama and most of the women from the village went on a day pilgrimage to a tiny church nestled in the high mountains to honor the saint during the yearly procession. From my hideout in the tree, I used to watch them climb up the steep mountain trail, wooden sticks in hand, singing. Mama had been particularly devoted to the saint ever since my little brother had fallen in the brazier, suffered major burns all over his body, and eventually recovered without a mark.

Mama wasn't aware of what I was doing with the finances, and I wasn't going to worry her by telling. She probably knew we weren't doing well. I had never been able to pull the wool over Mama's eyes. Ever. The situation was bleak, but neither of us talked about it. I figured sometimes it's better to suffer in silence, and hope circumstances might turn around, than to admit to failure.

Next morning I dropped her off at church. I lied and told her I had to get the line ready. I was still haunted by childhood images of her dragging herself on her knees down the church's isle. Before she flung open the car door, Mama looked me in the eyes, questioning, probing, but also with that innocent and childish demeanor that surfaced when her guard was down. Mama's frequent outbursts of bitterness were nothing more than her pent-up frustration and anger resulting from her difficult life. Perhaps the fact she could never mold me to her beliefs inflamed her even more. But I never took her terse words to heart, held no rancor toward her, and didn't mind being the depository of her turgid emotions. True, though, there were times I wanted to pounce at her.

At last, she said, "Don't worry. Things always have a way of working out. Just do good in life, help others, and don't expect anything. But don't do like me. Don't ever look back." Her words felt like a ray of sunshine on a dark day, even raised goose bumps of pleasure inside my chest. It occurred to me that mothers always know a great deal more than you think they do.

I watched her now through the dashboard window as she climbed up the church steps and disappeared inside the door. It was a cloudy, chilly February day. Maybe by noon the sun would break free, for the faint breath of approaching spring lingered in the air.

At the restaurant, I went through the daily opening routine absentmindedly, filling two pots with water and setting them on the stove's back burners while mulling over Mama's words. I don't know why, but I felt better. Things didn't look as bleak as before. The soft blue and yellow morning was rising as the sun peered from behind the clouds and shined on the window, its soothing rays spilling into an oblong square on the floor. Everything would be fine, and I'd better learn not to look back. No one can retrieve time. I removed the béchamel that had been simmering overnight on the pilot light. I flattened the dough for the focaccia. I called my major supplier in Sacramento: one wheel of Parmigiano, half a pecorino, two tubs of fresh mozzarella, one 32-ounce can of anchovies, capers, two cases of olive oil, and three fifty-pound sacks of Mandako flour.

Then I reached into the pocket of my checkered pants and extracted the crumpled number Jane had slipped me before she left. It would be lying to say I hadn't thought about her constantly since her surprise visit. I tried mighty hard not to give in to the thought of seeing her again. This wasn't right, my guilt whispered. She was a married woman now. It had puzzled me that I hadn't seen a ring on her finger. Maybe she'd taken it off temporarily. I'd wanted to ask her about it then, but couldn't bring myself to do it. She had been my girl once, and in my mind that entitled me to some special privileges.

Call me some time, she had scribbled on a paper napkin. As I traced my fingers over the letters I felt my heart race with excitement. Butterflies fluttered in my stomach. I remembered all the birthday cards Jane had given me over the years. Inside each one she had inserted a dry flower and drawn little smiling hearts. I still had them buried somewhere. There had been a time I was so much in love with her I ached from it.

I mustered the courage to call her and told her to come by on a Monday night for dinner.

When I went back to the church, I saw Mama waiting on the sidewalk, her purse dangling. Her black veil, the long, golden hair over which she had once worn it, and the striking beauty of her youth had all faded now, stolen by that thief: time.

I remembered the church in Milano I'd run into when I fled my first day of class, the pew where I'd cried my heart out for things that had seemed so important then, yet mattered not now. I could still hear the fruit vendor's cries as he worked behind his cart. *Apples! Pears! Oranges! Come on, women. Where else can you find such quality and value?* Other images intruded: waiting at the lonely bus station at ten o'clock after I got out of night school. Falling snow brightening the night sky, the Sforzesco castle across the street with its massive greenish stone walls somber and watchful like a sentinel of the night. Arriving home to eat whatever Mama had left on the table covered with the blue-checkered cloth.

Mama seemed unusually quiet in the car. I sensed something had happened and asked her about it. "Nothing," she said dismissively. She had a serene look on her face, as if something pleasant had taken place in church. Did she meet an acquaintance? A neighbor? What could have happened that she didn't want to share with me? Like an itch, I couldn't let it alone.

My impatience spilled out before I could hold it back. "So, you want to tell me what's the matter or what?" I had raised the tone of my voice, and immediately wished I could take those words back. But it was too late. She shifted in the seat and slowly turned to face me, her eyes piercing me.

I said nothing more.

When we got to the shop I tied an apron over my white jacket and began making chicken cannelloni. I deliberately stayed away from the traditional Italian menu. Lasagna, manicotti, cannelloni, and spaghetti and meatballs weren't even on it. I wanted people to start talking about all the new dishes we offered.

I always ran late to get the line ready. Between the menu and the specials there seemed to be a million things to prepare, even with Mama's help. I wished I had three pairs of hands. In this line of work, one pair never seemed enough.

I handed Mama a bowl of 16/20 prawns to peel. She scowled at me and sat on a chair at the table by the door, her back to me, Father Pio's little prayer book at her side. She hadn't said a word to me thus far. My guilt nudged me. Mixing family and business can make for unhappy moments. You can talk to a stranger candidly, but when it's family you have to play dumb. We both went about our business in silence.

Guilt played havoc with my mind. I knew I'd said or done something wrong, but whatever it was, it was too late to undo it now.

"I didn't mean to hurt your feelings," I whispered, sounding to myself like a ten-year-old. If I hadn't apologized, she wouldn't have talked to me for a week. And I couldn't handle seeing her in a *muso lungo*, a sulk, for that long. Her only response was a slight perk of her head. I kept going. If she wanted to answer, fine. If not, well, I'd done my part. But I itched to know what had happened. I stooped, picked five white onions from a burlap sack, and started peeling them.

"What a lousy way to talk to me," she suddenly blurted out, the chair creaking under her shifting weight. Her words were loaded with disappointment. Craning her neck, looking over her shoulder in my direction, her eyes inflamed with hurt, she said, "That's the thanks I get for all the tenderness and love I gave my first-born." My stomach tied into a knot. I kept silent, slicing the onions. Her words stung me with guilt. Burning tears pooled in my eyes and coursed down my cheeks.

"But even if I told you what happened," she resumed, her back to me, "you wouldn't believe me." I had no idea what she meant, but at least I'd got her talking now.

She finished peeling the prawns and stacked them in a neat row on the cutting board. Then she began butterflying them. She guided the point of the knife, gently peeling down the back of each crustacean, exposing the rich white meat.

"Well, tell me, and let me decide," I pleaded, sautéing the onions. "Did you forget I've got a mind?"

She put down the knife. Absentmindedly, she dried her hands on the towel hanging from the tie of her apron and then slowly turned to face me. Her eyes looked far off into space with contemplative interest, as though she was mulling over something, her lips parted. She lingered a few seconds, then, "I had a miracle in church," she said at last.

My heart skipped a beat. Was she serious? What miracle could she have had? Was she all right? I looked outside the shop's window, at the eyesore gas station view. I peeled my eyes away from it, disappointed, and studied Mama's face closely for clues that might make sense of all this. I forced myself to snap out of the stupor. "What miracle?" I said, my voice cracking.

She explained that in church, she'd lit a candle, knelt before the statue of a saint, and prayed. Then, suddenly, she'd felt a hand on her shoulder. Startled, she'd turned around. And seen no one. "I thought it was you at first, always in a hurry like *gli Americani*."

I shook my head and swallowed heavy air. I waited.

"I looked around the church, but it was empty." She paused, thinking. "Then I thought maybe there was some man who wanted to get fresh with me hiding somewhere. You know?" Her eyes lingered on me.

I didn't know. I couldn't imagine such a thing. I stared at her, trying not to laugh. Yet at the same time I was worried sick. She was normally so lucid. How could she come up with this nonsense? Could this searing summer heat be affecting her to such an extent? That she was seeing things? Guilt swept through me again. I wished I'd gone with her. "So, what did you do next?" I asked, dreading what she might say next as I sautéed the mixture of onions, celery, and yellow peppers that were to be the base for the cannelloni. Wisps of inviting aromas rose from the pan, and were swallowed by the hood's fan.

"I looked around the pews to see if anyone was hiding, but there was nobody."

I began to dice the cooked chicken meat. "And then what?" I asked, curious and anxious to see where it would all lead.

Mama considered.

"Then, I knew it was the Saint," she said with certainty and a little smile. "There was nobody there. Who else could it be? It was he who touched me. He has always answered my prayers." She shook her clasped hands and turned her moist eyes to the ceiling.

I knew she was referring to a time in Milano when, unable to endure life in Nonna's home any longer, she had entertained the thought of returning to Calabria. She had known there was no future for us there. And every day she went to church, lighted a candle, and begged the saint for a miracle. A few months later we were granted our own apartment.

I stared at her, wordless, as the memories of those painful and yet precious years surfaced again. Mama's chiseled face had hardly any wrinkles in it. Her cheeks glowed with a rose light. But now there was weariness in her eyes as though the years had clouded her once-keen expression. With a sinking heart, for the first time, I realized Mama was beginning to look old.

Suddenly, I remembered my near-death experience with the trolley in Milano. That morning, Mama had told me of a portentous dream she had during the night: someone had offered her sweets. Mama's life was guided by symbols she deciphered from her dreams. I'd sneered and brushed aside her premonition as nonsense. That same muggy summer evening, on my way to night school, I began absentmindedly crossing a street. And when I reached the middle of the road, I heard a clear voice in my head call out my name and tell me to stop and look to my right. When I tilted my head sideways, a silent tram sailed past, inches from my nose. This was the second time I'd been spared death by tram. Could this be the same power manifesting to Mama, bringing us closer together? I wondered whether something divine really had occurred to her in church.

I was beginning to believe that anything was possible.

GAMBERI ALL'AGRETTO

PRAWNS WITH LEMON

Serves 4

1 tablespoon olive oil, and one butter

12 oz sliced mushrooms of your choice

Salt to taste

20 16/20-size prawns

½ tablespoon minced garlic

1-2 oz dry white wine

Juice of one lemon

1 oz butter

2 tablespoons minced parsley

Peel, butterfly, de-vein, and pat dry the prawns. Set aside.

Heat oil and butter in large skillet over medium heat. Add mushrooms, and salt lightly. Cook 3 to 4 minutes. Add prawns, garlic. Deglaze with wine and let evaporate. Add lemon juice. Cook for about a minute. Adjust for salt and pepper. Add butter and parsley and serve at once.

SEVENTEEN

"I wouldn't worry about it. Just keep an eye on her. Maybe it's this wave of heat we're having that's affecting her. Just make sure she drinks plenty of fluids," Silvio said, sounding more like a physician than the schoolteacher he was.

Mama's anointing of the restaurant hadn't produced any changes. I confess that some part of me hoped it might. I couldn't get deeper into debt. The desire to work on my own was beginning to seem a distant dream. I blamed myself for my impatience and my insistence on doing things my way, but I was determined to hang on, by my nails if necessary, until every possibility was exhausted.

What worried me most was that Mama would crumble at the prospect of my life's savings disappearing completely—of seeing her son crushed under the weight of a failed venture. But I wasn't defeated: not yet. I remembered Nonna's adage, *Finche' c'e' vita c'e' speranza.* I was alive, yes, and there was still hope.

I'd asked Nonna to send me the recipes she'd been collecting over the years. I thumbed through them now, hoping to come up with new ideas and recipes, striving to be the most innovative cook in town. I called her every Sunday to keep her up to date on the progress of the business. I told her I wasn't doing well, but she said to hang in there because "No time can last forever, good or bad." Nonna ladled out her proverbs like divine sustenance. Every time we spoke she asked when we intended to return home. And every time, her question tore at my heart.

Shopping for food items locally was time-consuming. But I believed it was important to serve fresh, organic food as much as possible. In Calabria we raised practically everything we ate—which wasn't much. And then there was Milano. Food was so much part of the fabric of life in those places I couldn't have approached it any other way than to choose it with my own hands, inspect it with my discriminating eyes. It gave me enormous pleasure to trace my fingers over the rippling veins of a Napa cabbage, to observe the pink, live color of ground beef, and to feel the flat green leaves of Italian parsley crunch under the blade of my knife as I minced it. But for me the ultimate pleasure was knowing that we cooked with wholesome ingredients whose quality could not be surpassed anywhere.

Perhaps the reason I'm drawn to food, and feel such a deep awe and excitement in its proximity, is that there was so little of it growing up in Calabria. My deepest fear is that one day I may wake up and there won't be any more food left in the world. That's why I always serve and buy more food than necessary. As though stocking up on it is a guarantee that I will never experience hunger pains again.

Shopping Old-World style for food was not only gratifying, it allowed me to experiment with new ingredients, create new recipes, and stretch my creative boundaries. My love for pasta, the first food I remember eating, sometimes against my wishes for lack of a better choice, had remained a fascination of mine. And propelled by this, my thirst to discover the best items to compliment this universal noodle had become my secret and never ending quest. Over time I must have used endless scores of items to pair it with in my daily specials. Here are a few from the vegetable kingdom: sun-dried tomatoes, eggplant, zucchini, string beans, potatoes, morels, shitake, porcini, olives, artichoke, rapini, broccoli, radicchio, and even avocado. All of them good recipes. Some excellent. But I always returned to the simplest and most perfect ingredient which seemed to have been created to complement pasta. The tomato. This, and a simple garlic and oil sauce with a touch of *peperoncino* and parsley, still rank as my favorites.

However, as good as I was with food consistency in the kitchen, in my search for the perfect pasta dish, I discovered— to my amazement— that each dish always turned out a bit different than its predecessors. Using the same recipe, the same exact ingredients and quantities every time, was no guarantee for sameness. There was always a slight variation in each dish, a subtle difference. All variables created by the type of vegetable, season, and where it was grown. As though each and every dish had a life of its own, a character of its own, even a will of its own.

Nonetheless, I was always thinking, watching, searching for something that could approximate perfection in the kitchen, particularly with pasta dishes. But I was deluding myself, for a dish could never be duplicated, no matter how skillful and consistent a cook might be. For each creation is born out of the spontaneous moment—a moment that can never be relived, which lingers briefly before the eyes and then is gone in no time at all. This was the sad part about food; it didn't last, except for that brief ephemeral interval between preparation and consumption.

Our usual workday started around seven. After a quick espresso at home, Mama and I would hit the road. While I navigated the streets of Fresno Mama sat next to me, brainstorming specials for the coming weekend. And if she hadn't gotten much sleep—which was the case most nights— and her culinary juices weren't flowing, she invariably consulted the cook next to her. But since my brain was always groping for possible solutions to improve business, I told her I couldn't concentrate on specials while driving. This exonerated me. Most times.

Sometimes as we drove down the freeway, my hideout in the poplar tree flashed through my mind. Although now it was gone, inside my head it still lived.

Our first stop on Tuesday mornings was the downtown market, on Merced Street. We arrived like clockwork at seven thirty for our weekly ritual. I used to call it the little United Nations market on account of the babble of languages spoken amongst the stands.

Right across the street, cater-corner from Fresno's famous Water Tower, Mama had discovered a young bay laurel tree. She would reach up and grab a branch, raising herself on the soles of her feet, calf muscles taut, sometimes even showing a rim of her white undergarment in the process. Then, the branch clasped to her side like a subdued prisoner, she would pluck leaves at a furious pace. These she would dry for a few months to use in certain meat dishes like pork stew.

One day, after I had slammed the trunk on the day's load of fresh vegetables and was about to walk over and help her, I spotted a cop car parked at the tree. An officer was talking to her.

I ran.

Luckily, the officer was an acquaintance. He let us go with a warning not to be seen vandalizing city property again.

On rare occasions the market served as a place to exchange local gossip with a few compatriots. For instance: The new Italian restaurant that had opened in town. The speculation whether it would last, how well it might do. The latest deceased. A recent divorce, separation, or infidelity. Who bought a new car and paid cash. Or simply reminiscing about the virtues and faults of the old country.

The first time I took Mama with me to get tomatoes on the west side of town, she was shocked at the level of poverty she saw. Discarded tires, tattered sofas, and carcasses of dilapidated cars rested on wood or cement blocks in weed-strewn front yards. "Is this part of America?" she asked, wide-eyed. Over the years I'd gotten used to such sights, but I could never explain them. I suppose, in comparison to Mama, I'd become a little indifferent to them now. "I thought I knew what poverty was, but I guess I don't," she concluded.

We were usually at the restaurant by eight o'clock, after our last stop at La Boulangerie for baguettes. And compared to some kitchens I had worked in, which required me to be on the job by six in the morning, this felt like cheating.

While I unloaded the produce, Mama filled two pots of water, placed them on the stove, covered them, and turned on the flame. Covering the pots helped bring the water to a boil faster, and more importantly, saved on the gas bill. She used to shut off the flame under the skillets every time I stepped away from the stove to greet a customer or answer the telephone. I understood her reasoning, but coming back to my stove and seeing the food in the skillets had gone cold and limp drove me up the wall. And no matter how many times I told her not to mess with my sauté, my pleas always fell on deaf ears.

As if putting up with her eccentricities here wasn't enough, at home I had my father to deal with as well. He'd chase me around the house reminding me that I'd forgotten to turn off the light, wasting precious kilowatts.

They had unscrewed most of the light bulbs in the sockets of the light fixtures at home, leaving a single light bulb in each fixture so that if I had to read at night, I needed a flashlight. Sometimes I thought I was hallucinating, going back to my grandmother's time. Her extreme frugality was understandable, given the time and place. But now, in the twentieth century, in America? But really, they couldn't be blamed. The real culprit was the energy company, which would find a way to rip us off no matter how we scrimped.

Preparing focaccia was always my job, for Mama's fingers, although tough, weren't strong enough to break through the stubborn elasticity of cold dough. My years of martial arts training served me well as I pounded the dough with my open hands, to deflate it, worked and stretched it with my fingertips. Sometimes I even threw it up in the air, just to hear Mama grumble.

She pre-cooked a few orders of pasta, except for the *fettuccine* and *cappellini*, which cooked to order in minutes. She had the technique down perfectly. She submerged the pasta in boiling water until it was cooked *al dente*, then drained (never washed) and spread it on a sheet pan, where it was left to dry and cool. Prepared in this way, the pasta could be on a customer's table in minutes. Most restaurants, whether they admit it or not, use this method to meet the demands of the business in a timely manner.

When the pasta was ready, Mama watered the flowers on the windowsill with tender care, then swept the sidewalk with nearly as much vigor as my father.

The clock on the wall read nine sharp. Two more hours to lunchtime. It seemed like a long time, but it wasn't. The mushrooms had to be wiped one by one with a cloth, then sliced. The same for the scallions. Dicing the tomato and the butter came next, then chopping the garlic. I used a food processor for this, against Mama's wishes. She said it was a shame not to chop garlic by hand as needed, and correctly so. If I was cooking at home, for a small number of people, I would have done it her way.

Then came the specials. This caused conflict and debate, for Mama believed there was no reason to have more than two per day. But I, perhaps to appease the compulsions of my own mind, wanted four or five. And on weekends I liked to add two or three more, just to see her shake her head and murmur a string of Calabrian obscenities under her breath. In my previous positions, I would drive the servers out of their wits, demanding that each special be memorized.

Around ten thirty I peeked inside the proofer. The focaccia was nice and puffed—seven months pregnant, in human terms. In another ten minutes it'd be ready for delivery into the oven. Mama finished sweeping the sidewalk, took out the two rectangular plastic crates of colorful flowers, placed them on the windowsill, watered them with a plastic pitcher, and ran her fingertips over the flat top like you would tousle a child's hair. The town was slowly coming to life— the mailman handed Mama the day's mail, delivery trucks circled the center to enter the back lot, and the windows vibrated from the roar of throbbing engines.

Everything was right on schedule so far. I usually felt I deserved a quick cigarette break at this point, but with Mama in the area circling like a vulture, a smoke was out of the question.

Lunch was a breeze: ten to fifteen covers. I could have done it with one hand tied behind my back. A few orders of pasta, pasta salads, sandwiches, then more pasta salads and sandwiches. I figured if the trend continued, it wouldn't be long before I forgot what it was like cooking on the line and doing close to three hundred covers per night on weekends. Three hundred covers! I felt a surge of adrenaline course through me, and imagining the scent of a stack of twenty-dollar bills made my mouth water. I wished I could do less than a quarter of that business here.

The meatballs, when we made them every two weeks or so, were Mama's domain. Pouring spices into the cup of her hand, she regarded each item with calculating eyes before she tossed it into the mixture of ground meat in the dough mixer. And invariably she stood brooding over each batch like an alchemist waiting for a mysterious transformation to rise from the contents in the spinning bowl.

Our own lunch was in order, if time permitted. A plate of pasta in *bianco*, with oil or butter, and a generous sprinkle of Parmigiano for Mama. Or a tomato salad with sweet red onions, basil, oil. Or a simple *minestra* with a mélange of vegetables—our eating habits hadn't changed much since the days in Calabria. With her nervous stomach, Mama often lamented that now with God's *abondanza* surrounding her, she couldn't eat what she liked. Sometimes her nerves produced dreadful headaches: two pulsating peens hammering on her temples, as she described them. When the headaches were unbearable, which thank goodness wasn't often, Mama became completely dysfunctional. Then she would lie down on the couch in the dark living room with a damp cloth filled with slices of raw potato over her forehead. It was an old folk remedy, a crazy one, I think. Our doctor shook his head and told her that there was nothing physically wrong with her. It was nerves, he said, that's all. He patted Mama on the shoulder in consolation, told her not to worry. "But the pain. The pain, doctor. I wouldn't wish it on my worst enemy," she insisted. It's all nerves, he'd reply. And no amount of sedatives or cups of chamomile tea sweetened with honey seemed able to dispel her symptoms.

Once lunch was over it was time to start over again and get ready for dinner. And by the time Mama started the pinto beans to soak overnight for the minestrone and I wrote the next day's specials on the board, it was close to eleven o'clock. When we stepped out into the night with slouching shoulders and aching feet, I often thought, so much for the glorious restaurant life. I looked into the clear sky and took a breath of air, glad to leave behind the glare of fluorescent lights. Mama rattled the door handle half a dozen times, and at last nodded, satisfied that it was locked. And looking at the place from inside my pickup, it amazed me how much I had become part of it, and it part of me. It's scary how a man becomes what he does.

As the end of the season drew near I began dreading the prospect of having to cook with the sad, sterile, plastic-looking tomatoes of winter. My sauces wouldn't have the same rich flavor. I voiced my regret to Silvio, and through his friend Rosa, who worked for a big tomato ranch in Coalinga, we were invited to pick as many post-harvest tomatoes as we wanted.

This would allow me to dice them, bag them, freeze them, and use them in winter. Surely they would lose a great deal of flavor, but they would be much better than those tasteless rocks I hated with such passion. In my opinion, Italian food without good tomatoes is like a day without sunshine.

Worse.

Silvio and my father led the way in the blue Plymouth heading for Highway 180. Down the two-lane country road we went in the gray dawn, vineyards on either side, raisins drying on the ground along each row. I followed a short distance behind with Mama. Two carloads would last me awhile, I reasoned. The rest I'd put in specials, dice, add oregano, fresh basil, salt, and pepper, and drown in olive oil. I'd let them steep in a bowl for an hour or two, then serve them over a bed of hot pasta. It would make a tasty summer dish. I could oven roast a portion as well, and when I ran out later on, I'd try to locate top-of-the-line imported San Marzano tomatoes.

California grew great tomatoes, but the canning process loaded them with citric acid, which made them unpalatable and bitter. Even top-notch chefs will sometimes soften the sauces made from such tomatoes with sugar, but in my opinion this practice dulls and flattens their natural flavor, so in my kitchen, sugaring tomatoes is a no-no.

The sun looked like a ring of fire rising over the rim of the eastern hills as we approached the sprawling ranch. Ahead of us were endless, shadeless green fields.

Banana boxes and five-gallon buckets in hand, we set out on our tomato quest in the furrowed fields that succeed each other ad infinitum. The vines, a dwarf variety, lay half-trampled, many of the fruits crushed, as if careless feet had plowed through them in a great hurry. This field had hardly been picked. Tomatoes grew fat and luxurious under the blistering California sun. Thick clusters of five, ten, or more orange-sized tomatoes nestled in the dark, dew-damp earth.

The sight left us dumb with excitement. I trembled with pleasure and so did everyone else. Our exclamations of wonder broke the silence of the warm September morning. Like children discovering a hidden treasure, we could hardly contain our enthusiasm. We hopped about from one row to the next in search of ever bigger and more perfect fruit, all the while voicing mild regret for the ones we left behind. "Look at these," one of us would shout. We convened, admiring the harvest and filling our buckets. We shook our heads in disbelief at so much waste, discussing the possibility of returning with a U-haul truck the next day.

Mama stopped picking, straightened her back, and contemplated the fields in awe. "Are you sure this is legal?" she demanded. "Are you sure we're not in the wrong field?"

Silvio laughed and asked her if she wanted permission in writing. My father picked with quick, able hands, ferreting out the contents of the buckets and transferring them cautiously into boxes. Silvio and I stole a bite here and there, and before long were pelting each other with tomatoes like we used to do with snowballs in Milano.

"Don't you dare pick up those boxes," Mama suddenly blurted out to my father, as he was about to load one onto his shoulder and carry it to the car. "And you two. Stop monkeying around."

"We'll do it, Pa," I called out.

"You think you are still young? Eh? What's the matter with you?" Mama scowled at him. He frowned, shot her a disgusted look, and set off into the field again, bucket dangling from his hairy forearm.

Loaded with as much fruit as the cars could hold, we sat by a little canal drying the sweat and dust off our faces. I looked at Silvio's red-spattered T-shirt and laughed. We both looked like we had been through a firing squad. Our parents shook their heads in disapproval.

Mama spread a tablecloth on the ground. My father took a bottle of Barbera from the trunk, and I took out fresh mozzarella, a baguette, and a few packets of salt. I broke the bread and passed it around, then sliced the cheese. Father took a long gulp, and passed the bottle. Then he cut the tomatoes with his hooked harvest knife. Fat, rich, and dripping slices like beef medallions.

"What would you plant if you owned all this land?" I asked him, making a sweeping gesture over the field. He smiled as though I had asked a tricky question. I wondered if he could envision himself farming on such scale. I remembered reading one of several old love letters he had written to Mama while working in Milano—I'd found them years later buried inside a drawer. In it he declared his undying love for her; how he longed to return to Calabria and buy his own little plot of land. But that dream never materialized, for there was never enough money for such dreams. So his lot in life had always remained as small as the parcel of land in the back yard. He was a true peasant at heart. He cherished the land as something sacred and had spent almost his entire life cultivating it, caring for it, like it were a living creature. Father was bred for the land. And the irony of it all was that he hadn't ever owned any.

Father hauled himself to his feet. He strode to the edge of the field. His eyes strayed to the front rows. His black hair had turned nearly all gray and glittered in the sunlight. Now in his mid seventies, he still looked strong and limber. He stooped and plucked a ripe tomato. He wiped it with quick movements up and down his checkered gray shirt. He held it in the palm of his hand. His eyes lingered on it with satisfaction. It was so big and luscious. We could dry pounds of them in the sun, I thought. "Nobody owns the land," he said, turning to me. "Nobody."

Leaving the Alfa Romeo plant where he had worked on the assembly line for close to twenty years and coming to America had been a big change for my father. But although he rarely expressed his feelings, he was in awe of this country and regretted not having migrated here in his younger days. He too must have seen the possibilities, the allure of it all.

But never a man with big dreams, Father seemed to be always content with the small things in life. Leave the fancy and pretense of life to others, and let him steep in the simple things. The real, pure things life offered free for the taking. He would look into a fresh-squeezed glass of grape juice at harvest season and refer to it as God's milk and honey. Or he would pour his efforts into his vegetable garden—his life's passion—where he'd hunker down on his knees and watch a tiny vegetable stalk grow, his sun-bronzed face glowing with all the wonder of a child looking at the moon. Did he wonder whether the labor of his hands was responsible for such a miracle? If he did, I never knew it. Father was a man of few words. I never remember the two of us having a man-to-man conversation. I sure missed that.

Mama chimed in. "This owning business is all man's invention, as far as I am concerned," she announced sagely to the air.

Silvio looked at me and winked.

"God never said that some of us can own it, and others can't," Mama concluded with a flurry of passion. "The land belongs to everyone." Then she lowered her head and sprinkled too much salt on her mozzarella.

Father grinned. He was an anomaly for a Calabrian man. He never laid a finger on Mama. Never told her to shut her mouth. Never acted as though she was his possession, his servant. Never embarrassed nor humiliated her in front of strangers, or in private, unlike most Calabrian men I knew. He even helped her with house chores—mopping the floor on

Sundays, shopping when she wasn't well, something unusual for a Southern Italian man, who expected his wife to wait on him like a king, as if he held the power of her life and death in his hands. The only downside to Father was his explosive temper, which he always dissipated by tending his garden, gulping a glass or two of Barbera, soaping and scrubbing his hands raw. Now he looked at her and half smiled. His eyes filled with pride. This was his woman, who had stood by him in good times and in bad. She was the type of woman he liked. She was considerate, loving, and patient. A frugal wife who knew how to stretch a dollar beyond its limits, and who waited on him hand and foot. But when her temper flared, he disappeared.

In her younger years she had been the envy of the village. Suitors flocked to her like bees to a flower for her great beauty. One suitor was a senator all the way from Rome. Father could hardly believe she'd refused a senator's proposal and chosen him instead. My parents had been shipmates on the rough seas of life. And neither one of them would have had it any other way, so binding was their love for each other.

Mama took a bite of her tomato stack. Her glowing eyes scanned the fields again. "It sure is a blessed land, though," she whispered to no one.

Both cars were filled to the brim. We flooded the trunks, the back seats, and every inch of space we could find, until tomatoes reigned supreme, and the vehicles sagged.

Father stood at the edge of the field near a telephone pole that cast a long shadow. He had picked up a handful of dry brown soil, and was letting it pour between his fingers, staring at it as if it were gold flakes slipping from his hand, dissipating into the ground. "If I could only have had a small parcel of this…" I could imagine and hear his words inside my head. Despite Mama's calls, he solemnly contemplated the fields as we waited inside the idling vehicles.

There seemed to be no better place in the world, I thought. The relentless beating sun shimmered and burned over the jagged, baked hills in the distance. A light wind rose and rippled across the open plains like a wave. It shivered the tomato vines, brought forth the scent of the rich soil, the fragrance of the cultivated land. This was no ordinary beauty one could ignore. It set my heart racing, gripped my stomach with a pang of pleasure, and in the end, left me a little breathless.

The stillness that reigned over the plains seemed like an exhalation that stretched into eternity. Mama's shrill calls seemed to profane the sanctity of the moment, the peacefulness of time and space.

Father slammed the Plymouth's door shut, rested his shoulder against the seat, and looked at his watch.

I knew what he would plant, if he owned the land.

SPAGHETTI AI TRULLI

SPAGHETTI, TRULLI STYLE

Serves 4

This, more than any other dish, embodies the simplicity and earthiness that typifies the cuisine of southern Italy.

16-20 oz diced, garden-ripe tomatoes	*3-4 oz olive oil*
2-3 tablespoons minced fresh garlic	*Basil, 10-12 leaves*
	Salt and ground pepper to taste
Oregano to taste	*1 lb of pasta*

Wash, dry, and dice tomatoes. Put them into medium-size bowl (please, no plastic).

Add garlic, oregano, oil, salt and pepper to taste. Mince and add the basil. Mix well with a spoon. Adjust for salt and pepper. Cover with a towel, and let it steep at least 30 minutes at room temperature.

In a pot of boiling water, cook your favorite pasta, as per previous instructions. Drain and pour pasta into a large deep platter. Add tomato sauce over hot pasta. Toss, add some more fresh minced basil, more oil to taste. Serve.

EIGHTEEN

Mama and I worked side by side scraping mussels, peeling garlic, and dicing our Coalinga tomatoes. A chef in Milano taught me that if a tomato is perfect and sun ripened, the entire fruit can be used. With a great tomato, something as ordinary as pasta can, with the addition of a few other ingredients, be transformed and elevated into something approaching art, and in only a matter of minutes. This is the beauty of Italian cuisine, and true to this philosophy, we believed that if we offered such food, eventually people would come.

As we worked in the kitchen with the stereo playing, sometimes Mama's eyes would overflow with tears listening to songs from a time when she had no idea that one day she would end up working her own restaurant in America. But these were also tears for the people she had left behind, for a land she still missed, for its memories she cherished, and for a world that had become distant and hazy, as though it had never existed. The restaurant was our first claim to the American dream. As we worked together, I learned she had great business intuition, including an uncanny ability to sense what customers wanted. My knowledge was theoretical, hers intuitive. "Sometimes you can't go by the book," she said. *E' tutto qui'*, she would insist, slapping her stomach, reminding me that gut feelings sometimes are the best compass with which to navigate life. In particular, she pounded me to increase the pasta portions. I had learned strict portion control everywhere I had worked, but I gave in a little, and under Mama's influence the plates grew larger by the day until pasta was heaped like pyramids.

Our small clientele raved. Perhaps Mama did know best.

The health inspector came in every three months for routine inspection, and when Mama was present, she would sometimes ask me to prepare something for him. "Make him something good. Ask him what he likes." But everyone always politely refused any offerings. It was difficult for Mama to believe such a behavior —and long before, I did too. She'd just shake her head in disbelief. Later, she'd stand in the doorway and cast furtive glances at the inspector while, locked inside his car, he munched on a cold sandwich. "Not like them vultures back home. Look at the poor man, for God's sake! Why doesn't he want to take something warm instead? Here is too much one way. In Italy too much the other way," she'd opine, then hobble away, perplexed.

Under Mama's watchful eye nothing went to waste. Scraps of veal trimmings, a prosciutto bone, a pork cutlet too small to serve, chicken carcasses with dangling gizzards and livers: all became, with the addition of celery, carrots, and onions, hearty soups.

Mama protested that the abundance and excess of America had gone to my head, numbed my senses, and made me forget the times when, in order to make ends meet, she used to prepare me boiled chicken feet for lunch.

How could I ever forget that?

But the soups were a reminder of cold winter nights sitting at Nonna's long dining room table while the rain battered the windows and the wind rattled the shutters like a vengeful demon. Everyone at the table voiced their opinions on the topics of the day amidst the clatter of silverware. I tried to savor each bite while attending to all of the loud conversations at once, and sometimes I scalded my tongue while contemplating that one day these moments would become only faint memories.

I'd no doubt that if Mama had been thrust into a different life, she could have turned loose her ambitions, would have achieved anything she had set out to do. Unlike my father, she had an innate sense of curiosity, and a creative force bottled up inside her that cried out to be expressed. Whether she was aware of these qualities remains a mystery to me. But some days they shined like daylight through the windows of her soul. It saddened me to think she could have been so much more, had she not devoted her life solely to her family and her faith.

Mama was appalled at the plates she brought back from the tables, some half full, others unfinished, focaccia untouched. Her eyes widened in disbelief at so much waste. Sometimes she would bring a slice of bread to her lips, kiss it, offer it to the sky, and moan, "Oh, *Dio*, if I had this during the war I would have wept. Many a night I cried myself to sleep with hunger. It's a sin to throw food away. There are children in the world going to bed hungry every night." Mama always lingered by the garbage pail, her sad eyes staring at the basket in her hand, and kissed the bread each time before she tossed it.

I remembered the little black notebook smeared with oil smudges Mama used to give me to buy bread on credit at the *panettiere*. Father would pay his debt at the end of the month. I could only imagine what Mama must have felt now, each time before she tossed bread into the trash. Eventually we befriended a customer who raised chickens. Then Mama's heart didn't ache so much anymore.

She abhorred waste of any kind. More than my father, who had been born to a well-to-do family. But there was no striking difference between my parents in their habit of saving unimaginable items for posterity. They stashed away egg cartons, grocery bags, pens, cardboard boxes, and new towels to last us the next hundred years, not to mention twenty-year-old shoes, jackets, shirts, and pullovers. If the Salvation Army were to depend on my parents' contributions, it would be history.

They never threw anything away.

Mama pointed out that I had become American because I spent too much money on things that weren't necessary. For instance, she thought my three hundred pairs of jockeys, five hundred pairs of socks, and multiple daily showers unreasonable.

If I had to pick the two things I loved most about America, I would have to pick its open plains, and its showers. Yes, showers. My compatriots could build Ferraris, mile-long tunnels through the Alps, aqueducts, spectacular bridges, and the Colosseum, but they can't build a shower like Americans can—they probably never will either. Every time I went to Europe, and Italy in particular, I was livid that I couldn't take a decent shower without inundating the floor, or contorting myself like a trapeze artist trying to spray water on my body. Mama thought I took too many showers now. Good. Let her think so. I was vindicating myself for all those years when we didn't have one.

But considering the life Mama had endured in Calabria, her behavior wasn't surprising. No electricity, no running water, no stove, no heat, hardly any food to eat. Giving life to each one of us in that shack with no doctor, only an arrogant midwife who arrived late on each occasion, on a donkey's back, in the middle of the night, disheveled, acting like she was Queen Elisabeth, in Nonna's words.

No wonder Mama thought I was spoiled.

Sometimes when I overheard Aunt Mary describe to her American friends how hard life was in Calabria, I knew that no one could ever understand her remark, the true meaning of those words.

Hard, I felt like saying.

One Monday night, when my brother stopped at the restaurant after teaching all day, I told him there was no need for Mama to stay late. Business had been slow, and there were still five remaining cases of tomatoes that Mama had to can. This was a yearly ritual she had adhered to ever since I can remember.

The jars would first be boiled in water to sterilize them. Then they were filled with halves of tomato which had been strained of seeds and excess water. She'd press the chunks firmly into each jar to avoid air pockets, add basil leaves, and cap them. Boiling them for about half an hour completed the process.

Mama eyed me suspiciously, as though she could feel something out of the ordinary in my behavior, and protested that closing was too much work for one person. But when I reminded her of the tomatoes sitting in the heat on the back porch at home, she offered no more resistance. It was ten to eight. Dinner had been another disaster. I had passed out fliers in the neighborhood in the morning—and been chased by a mean stray dog—hoping to drum up some business, but only three deuces had showed up all evening. During the last hour not a soul had come in. My heart sank. I felt like getting drunk or running away to the hills.

The call of the mountains still drew me. Sitting in the green plastic chair outside the restaurant, I used to stare toward distant Yosemite. Every chance I got I drove near it, even for half a day, sat on the lake shore, and bathed in its stillness and silence—this had become my new hideout. I never found *porcini*, though. Some of the local old-timers brought me a package from time to time, but they never shared their secret spots.

It was invigorating to breathe the crisp mountain air, peel a sliver of bark from a tree trunk, or smile at a darting jackrabbit. Over time I had even built a small wooden cabin in the woods of my imagination. A place I escaped to in moments of frustration like these. But then I remembered the ulterior motive for sending Mama away and my outlook brightened. Jane was coming. She would show up at any moment—not in the cabin of my dreams, but here, in my restaurant. A smile sprouted on my lips.

I had been floating on clouds all day with the mere thought of seeing Jane again. I even gave out the wrong change a few times, to Mama's dismay, as thoughts of love wafted through my head. She had wrinkled up her nose like a rabbit several times, as if she sniffed imminent sin. Possibly even lust. And knowing her radar-like sensitivity, it wouldn't have surprised me if she could read my thoughts like an X-ray machine.

Huffing and puffing, Mama snapped open a large brown paper bag and filled it with focaccia bread, a leftover take-out order someone hadn't picked up, and a few other items from the cold box. This was one of the privileges and great advantages of owning a food business: getting groceries at wholesale prices. And one great consolation was that if things ever got bad enough, you could always eat your way to bankruptcy, or in the worst scenario, drink your way to oblivion, unlike many other types of business. Meanwhile,

I'd whipped up an order for my brother to take to school as his lunch. And out the door to the Plymouth parked by the curb I escorted them, while majestic arias played inside my head.

Jane arrived at eight thirty. She looked stunning, wearing an orange sweater with short sleeves, cut in a low V and tucked inside her jeans. The gold chain I'd given her on her nineteenth birthday glittered between her breasts. A small brown bag hung from her shoulder. In my head, I ran to her, wrapped my arms around her waist, and kissed her.

I motioned her to sit at one of the tables closest to the kitchen. This table was reserved for friends and family.

"Where is your mother?" she enquired, glancing toward the kitchen. She sat down and deposited her purse on the chair behind her. "I thought we were supposed to have dinner."

"We are," I said, grinning, and sat down next to her.

She raised a suspicious eyebrow and offered me a diffident smirk.

I told her about the tomatoes.

"She still doing that?" She slid her chair closer to mine, her eyes half-lidded.

I nodded. The past drifted back to me like a turning page as I watched the tanned high cheekbones my lips had kissed countless times. Age lines had formed around her ocean-blue eyes. I studied the soft contours of the face I had been so much in love with once that the rest of the world hadn't seemed to exist. The images of those exhilarating and painful moments surfaced again: images that had refused to be buried by time.

There were no more customers, no orders to go to fill. It was nine o'clock. I locked the front door and shut off the light in the dining room. The place seemed cooler now. The light spilling from the kitchen produced an intimate setting. A bouquet of red and yellow roses inside the glass vase on the table inspired romance. The night ahead seemed endless. My heart pounded with excitement.

I restarted Pavarotti's tape on the boom box, then returned to the table. "So, what shall it be, Ma'am?" I said in a grave tone. She giggled and threw her hands up. She gave me her usual smile: blatant, innocent, inviting.

"Anything. As long as there are no anchovies. Aren't you going to eat too?"

Ordinarily, I wouldn't eat my own food. The aromas from cooking it every day were sufficient to fill me. On those rare occasions when Mama didn't cook at home, I would get a burger, a burrito, or one of Di Cicco's *calzone*. I missed the great places to eat in San Francisco. But I couldn't let her eat alone. "Yes, and I'll have a big plate of anchovies. Medium rare, as appetizer." She laughed.

I got a bottle of Father's private reserve of Biola Barbera and poured each of us a glass. "To this pleasant surprise," I said, clinking her glass. She smiled. It all felt so good—almost like the old days. There was not a trace of guilt anywhere in me, knowing, as I now did, that she was divorced.

In the kitchen, I sliced prosciutto, *coppa*, and mixed cheeses. I poured kalamata olives into a bowl, cut half a baguette and made bruschetta.

"Take it easy," said Jane, hovering close and peering over my shoulder, watching me slice tomatoes. She patted her flat stomach. "I've got to watch my calories, you know." Her warm breath tickled the skin on my neck. Suddenly she laid a hand on my shoulder, leaned forward watching me layer tomatoes on baguette. Sparks of fire raced through me. A glowing sensation spread all over my body. I wanted to drop everything, turn around, and kiss her. I wondered how long I could resist the urge.

We went back to the table, plates in hand, to eat and drink in the semidarkness. Traffic whispered by outside on the street. Occasionally pedestrians walked by on the sidewalk, headed to the market. Some stopped to admire the long strands of pasta that hung in the front window like a curtain. "I can't believe this is happening," she said, chewing with gusto.

"I know," I mumbled, tasting too much garlic on the bruschetta. Given my state of mind I should have been thankful to make anything.

"So, things didn't work out between the two of you?" I knew I had ventured into dangerous territory by referring to her ex-husband, and I heard a tinge of resentment in my own voice. She could have been my woman if things had turned out differently. After all, I had loved her: loved her like no one before or since.

"Obviously not," she said, disappointment in her voice. She put down her fork on the placemat and pressed her back to the chair, brooding.

"I didn't mean to pry," I said, regretting having opened that can of worms. I should have kept my mouth shut.

"No, you didn't," she said after a long silence. "That's just how life goes. You think you've got somebody figured out, and then one day you realize you've been living with a stranger."

"How about a plate of pasta," I said, trying to break the seriousness of the moment. "And I don't want to hear about any calories tonight." I pressed my hands to my ears. She laughed. I couldn't believe how fast time was moving. The golden hands of the clock on the wall gleamed in the penumbra. It was ten-fifteen. By this time I would ordinarily be home. But tonight I didn't want to go to my empty room and stare at the dark. I wanted to be with her. I remembered the night I'd met her. I was twenty-three. We met, of all places, in a mirror. She was having a cocktail in a bar with her father. I sat three stools down. She'd materialized like an apparition, her eyes staring into mine in the mirror's reflection. It seemed ages ago now. I wondered if I'd have lived my life any differently. Probably not.

I remembered I still had to clean the kitchen, sweep and mop the floor, check out the register, and call in the Tuesday fish order. This jerked me out of my reverie.

She agreed to a popular dish on the menu: chicken breast, mushrooms, and peas, tossed with *pappardelle*.

We'd make it together.

"Can you get me some flour?" I handed her an empty take-out container and pointed to the sack. She took it and smiled. "I should have you teach me some tricks for home." I told her I was available. She giggled again and began digging into the flour.

I got a chicken breast, sliced it in half, then julienned it. I washed the knife and my hands, then placed a skillet on a burner and turned the knob. The flame curled around the pan. As I poured an ounce of clarified butter into the skillet, I tilted my head sideways to look at Jane's well-formed behind.

"Here. Is this okay?" She held out the flour. I nodded, reached out to get it, but it slipped through my oily fingers and splashed onto the floor, a cloud of white rising. We both stepped back and laughed as she slapped her hands clean. We squatted down to retrieve it, and almost butted heads. Being so close, I couldn't resist her anymore. I leaned forward and our lips met. We balanced, leaning against each other, and almost fell onto the floor. I smelled something burning while we kissed. Out of the corner of my eye I saw the skillet flicker with fire. I reached over and turned off the stove.

The stars gleamed distant in the clear sky. Jane leaned her head into my shoulder on the kitchen floor blanketed with a checkered tablecloth and pillowed with crumpled red napkins. The bottle of Asti Cinzano at my side sat almost full. There was no more need for champagne tonight.

The phone rang. Who could it be besides Mama? I jumped to my feet, ran, and squinted at the clock in the dining room. *Damn.* It was past eleven. It must be her for sure. I ran back to the kitchen, almost losing my red-striped boxers on the way. "Sshhhh," I whispered to Jane. "It's probably my mother." She raised her body on her elbows and stared. I bolted to the corner of the kitchen and switched on the dough mixer. Jane's eyes followed me, stupefied. Then I ran to the phone in the dining room, flicking the switch on the side of the hood in passing. It started with a violent whine followed by a gurgling rumble. One of these days the motor would blow for sure. Dollar signs flashed in my head. I made a sharp right turn, reached over, and started a Mario Lanza tape on the stereo. I cranked the volume. By the time I reached the phone on the wall, the place rocked with noise.

"Hello," I said, picking up the receiver, almost panting. It was Mama, demanding to know why I had taken so long to answer the phone. "Was busy cooking. Yes. Got a big party at the last minute. Eight of them." I could hardly hear her with the music so loud. Jane stood silhouetted by the back door, smoking. She still looked beautiful. "I know, but they requested it this loud." I adjusted my boxers with my free hand. "I've got everything cleaned up already, Ma. Don't wait up for me." I remembered the nights I used to go out with friends, come home late. Mama would be waiting for me, half asleep, hair undone, livid about my tardiness. More than two decades later, she was still waiting. Suddenly I caught sight of a man outside peering into the store, and crouched low to the floor against the display case. "They are busy eating. That's why they aren't talking, Ma. Look, I've got to go. They are asking for the ticket now. *Si, si*. Okay. Don't wait up for me. *Ciao*."

"You are going straight to hell for lying to that poor woman," Jane said, as I turned everything off and the place became quiet again. "Why can't you tell her the truth? Do you think she is so stupid she can't figure things out just because she doesn't understand English?" A long silence followed. A whisper of guilt stirred in me. The night lingered, peaceful and still.

I shut my eyes.

My feet dangle from my hideout in the tree. The goats graze below, nibbling at tender juniper leaves and anything they can reach by stretching their supple necks. One of the goats is slowly wandering off limits toward my uncle Dominick's vineyard below the hill slope. I curl my thumb and forefinger, stick them over my tongue. Whistle. The goat stops, turns, and just stares at me, his big ears flopping to the side. Stares as if he is trying to read my thoughts. Then resumes his path. I hate doing this. But I have no other alternative beside climbing down the tree trunk and running after him. I lift my shirt and extract my slingshot. Reach into my pocket for a smooth, round rock. I load it into the leather pocket. My right thumb and forefinger holding it tight, I point it at the goat's flank. Take aim. Let it go. The goat flinches. Now he trudges back, his head down, ears dangling. I tell him that's the price for disobeying as he nears the tree. I keep explaining myself, hoping my guilt won't last long. Then I toss him a sugar cube, so he knows that I'm not mean. Just the boss.

I opened my eyes.

Jane's back was pressing against my chest. I could hear someone outside rummaging in the dumpster. Probably the homeless looking for food. Go figure.

"You know my mother wouldn't approve of this," I said. "And I don't want to hurt her anymore. She was heartbroken when you left, in case you didn't know it."

Jane turned. Her eyes widened and fell on me. She sat up and wrapped her long fingers over her knees. "She was?"

I nodded. "That's right."

"I didn't know she cared that much for me."

"Well, you never gave her a chance. You just stormed out like you were on fire."

"I did *not*."

"You forgot, but you did," I said, wagging a finger at her and smiling. "Even if it was the wrong fire."

Her lips parted into a soft smile. "I have changed now. You know? I wish I could go back. I wouldn't make the same mistake. I guess you've got to lose something to value it."

Jane wove her fingers through mine, squeezed my hand, leaned over, and brushed her lips against mine.

"Do you ever wonder about timing?" she asked.

I had certainly thought about how our lives might have turned out had we not gone our separate ways. I watched her as soft gray light fell on her cheek. It occurred to me that this wasn't the casual teenager I once knew. This was a mature adult. I reached out and stroked her forehead, her hair.

"Do you ever wonder what it all means?" she said, staring through the transom toward a wedge of gray sky.

Strange, I had been asking myself these very questions ever since I could think. I curled my arms around her back, buried my face in her hair, and held her tight. I closed my eyes and let the past come back to me as I savored the tenderness of Jane lying next to me again. It occurred to me that a woman's love for a man could make his life worth living after all.

PAPPARDELLE CAMPAGNOLA

COUNTRY-STYLE PAPPARDELLE

Serves 4

This was a favorite at the restaurant over the years.

2 tablespoons olive oil

2 tablespoons unsalted butter

12-14 oz chicken breast, julienned

8 oz sliced button mushrooms

3 teaspoons minced garlic

2 oz dry white wine

2-3 medium ripe tomatoes, diced

6 oz frozen peas, thawed and rinsed

3-4 oz marinara sauce

2-3 oz cream

Salt and pepper to taste

2 tablespoons minced parsley

1 cup all-purpose flour

1 pound pappardelle

Remove skin from two chicken breasts of approximately 8 oz each. Cut each breast in half. Julienne each half, and set aside. Wash knife, the chopping board, and hands.

In a large skillet, heat the oil and butter over medium heat. Lightly coat the chicken strips with flour and shake them to remove excess. Lower meat into skillet and cook for about 10 seconds on each side. Remove with tongs and set onto platter. When finished, add mushrooms to skillet. Cook 3-4 minutes.

Add chicken again, follow with garlic. Deglaze with wine. Let it evaporate. Add diced tomatoes and peas. Toss. Salt and pepper to taste. Add marinara sauce and cream. Let it incorporate and simmer for a minute or so. If sauce looks too dry, add a little water from the pot where that pound of pappardelle should be cooking by now.

When pasta is ready, drain and add to skillet. Let it absorb the sauce for about half a minute. Add parsley. Serve piping hot.

NINETEEN

Uncle Frank came to visit us. He arrived on a searing August day. We all went to the airport to greet him. Mama was ecstatic, and so was I. It seemed unreal to see him out of his poker game surroundings, his daily routine at the shop, as he got off the plane wearing a light blue tailored shirt and cool white linen trousers. There were tears of happiness in his eyes as we hugged. The bicycle, the butcher shop, those Sunday excursions, and all the years came rushing back through me like a gust of wind. The old bond that existed between us quickly reemerged, as though time could never take it away. This was the first time he had gone out of the country—the last, too. What little hair was left on his head had turned gray. He looked a bit like grandfather now, with graying eyelashes and puffy eyes.

Outside the airport, the heat bore down on the asphalt. Uncle didn't seem to mind the 106-degree weather at all. He walked along with one arm wrapped around Mama's shoulder, the other over mine. At the parking lot, his eyes inspected my Cadillac with admiration and surprise. Then he grinned, drew me closer to him, and commented "*Americano, eh?*" I told him it was a rental. "No?" He shook his head in disbelief. He couldn't fathom that such cars could be rented. I reminded him that we weren't in Italy, where to rent a vehicle of this caliber you had to mortgage your house. He playfully slapped my shoulder.

He sat up front with me, his hand feeling the plush burgundy leather seat, looking wide-eyed at the dashboard with all its gadgets, many of which I didn't even know how to operate. I turned on the air conditioner full blast. From the back seat Mama complained that these drastic temperature fluctuations weren't good for the lungs. Uncle smiled and winked at me. There was no need to guess he approved of America. It was written all over his face like a child at the sight of a new toy.

That evening a long table was set up under the cottonwood tree. Mama spent hours in the kitchen preparing her stuffed red and yellow bell peppers and a pan of baked ziti with tomato sauce and tiny meatballs—her brother's favorite dish. She even fried *zeppole*—dough filled with anchovies—for the occasion, and a version without the filling sprinkled with powder sugar for dessert. Things she usually made for Christmas. I wouldn't have been surprised if she had expressed interest in cooking *Baccalà* salted cod, also a holiday specialty. I was in charge of the barbecue. I kept reminding myself that this was a real event, that Uncle was here, and that I wasn't dreaming. Old emotions resurfaced. Suddenly the house took on a new aspect—infused with Uncle's presence, it became more inviting, alive, meaningful. Mama showed him around each room, and Uncle's eyes grew wide at the sight of the whirling ceiling fans, the large kitchen, the 32-inch television set, the new burgundy carpet...

In the backyard, among the savory, smoky aromas of meat roasting on the barbecue, clinking glasses of red wine, and laughter, we recounted the old life in Milano.

Silvio took out his guitar and began singing Grandfather's songs. His fingers on the strings, and his warm voice rising in the purple dusk, awakened the neighbor's old dog and set the animal barking. Soon, Mama announced grace, and we all held hands around the table. And when the *antipasti* and first courses were over, I served the New York steaks. Uncle's eyes bulged. Once he had tasted it, however, he insisted that the meat from his shop had more flavor.

Two spotlights flooded the yard and cast balloon-shaped shadows under the tree. Dinner now over, Mama sat near Uncle, held his hand, and glowed in his presence. The heat lingered heavy in the night air, and as the coals in the barbecue slowly expired, cold beer took precedence over the wine. The stories became more intimate and drawn out over dessert. I had made a tray of tiramisu, which I'd placed in the freezer to really cool off. The music slowly faded, the night grew cooler and darker. The tall row of string beans beyond the table looked black in the shadows. It felt good to bask in the warm stream of companionship and affection that Uncle seemed to have revived in each of us. It was as though a fresh wind had blown it across the Atlantic and brought it among us. Perhaps this was a reminder that the old country hadn't forgotten us, that we hadn't been disowned for leaving her. Soon tiny stars appeared and twinkled in the slice of sky above. I remembered the falling star of my childhood, and wondered why I'd never seen another one.

Silvio took Uncle to Bodie, a ghost town on the California-Nevada border. Uncle was a die-hard fan of the old West. Then he took him to San Francisco because I couldn't leave my post in the kitchen. I'd given Silvio extra money to treat Uncle first class with food and lodging. They ended up spending the two days and evenings in North Beach. During the day they socialized with a bunch of countrymen at some little hole in the wall, playing cards and discussing fishing and politics. At night, they slept at some mediocre hotel in the Tenderloin district.

On the way back into the Valley, Silvio stopped at Gallo. But surprisingly, the winery didn't offer tours. So much for wanting to show Uncle some of his most successful countrymen in America.

As he got ready to board the plane back to Italy, Uncle confided to me that I'd given him the best time of his life. Then he smiled, and slid his hand along the rim of the black cowboy hat he had bought in Nevada. He told me that I'd been right to listen to my hunches, for America was truly beautiful. I believe that those three weeks were as good for me as they had been for him, and I was glad to have contributed a little happiness to his life—a small gesture considering all he had done for me over the years.

Almost every night before we closed up shop, Mama would bow in front of the crucifix in the kitchen and mutter a quick prayer. Sometimes she just stood solemnly, hands clasped, too tired to kneel.

The crucifix was such a familiar sight. I remembered it hanging above my bed in Milano, watching over my dreams. One hung in the kitchen to bless the food and the cook. One above the front door to look after our safe return home. And a tiny gold cross hung from a chain around my neck. Nonna had given it to me for guidance and protection.

A wave of guilt swept over me as I listened to Mama's words. I hadn't practiced any of those acts of faith in a long time. These were prayers she'd instilled in me with faith and devotion. I still wondered whether anyone could hear her supplications, or whether her words just dissipated into the night air and faded in the clouds.

Unbeknownst to Mama, I went to church. I dropped off an order of gnocchi and a bruschetta for Father Negri. I hadn't been to church in years, and I felt like the biggest hypocrite in the world turning to the church for help only in desperate times. It was a somber, drizzling winter morning. The rain pattered gently among the trees outside the church. The lawn was soaked. Small rivulets escaped into low ground and trickled over the curb into a gutter with a soothing, gurgling sound. A few lazy, fleecy clouds drifted across the gray sky. Another season would soon arrive, then pass away. One less spring to be enjoyed, to be lived. As I entered, a whiff of cool but stale air penetrated my nostrils. A handful of dark figures sat or knelt in the sanctuary. Compared to the grandiose and ornate cathedral in Milano, this little church seemed almost naked.

I dipped my fingertips into the holy water in the marble font by the door, glanced at the high altar, bent at the waist, and made the sign of the cross. Then I walked over to the statue of Saint Anthony, dropped a few coins into the offering box, lighted a candle, and placed it next to the other burning votives. The candle's flame flickered for a moment, then slowly settled, its spear of light pointing heavenward as though it anticipated my supplicating mood.

I got down on my knees.

The sweet smell of incense perfumed the semi-dark church. A faint stream of light filtered through the multicolored windows and splashed onto a row of pews. I shut my eyes, laced my fingers, and bowed my head. I remembered Mama kneeling by me at her bedside, my kneecaps aching on the damp floor, the chattering of frogs outside filling the quiet night. I remembered my innocent question of whether God could hear us. "*Dio* hears and sees everything," she had answered, her voice full of the conviction of a heartfelt faith. That was a quality that had been out of my reach, a concept my mind struggled to understand.

Sometimes I envied Mama's unrelenting certainty.

I opened my eyes and looked up at the statue, with the rows of burning candles at its feet swaying gently like a wave of fire. For an instant, Dante's *Inferno* flashed in my head. But the statue seemed to smile and glow with hope, the quality I needed most. Inside my head, I could see only saints with set faces and admonishing glances, scowling at me for my lack of faith. But this was the place where lost men like me came seeking hope. This was the house of God. And I knew He was a merciful, benevolent, and forgiving God. How could I not have believed in Mama's words? The time had come to cast aside my doubts. If my life had been spared twice, there must have been a reason, a purpose. There had to be. And to have come this far, after having endured so much, and now fail at my biggest endeavor—how could a loving God allow it?

I said, "Oh, God, I beg you, help me to make it." Then I remembered I hadn't truly prayed in a long time, except for a hurried request now and then in times of need. I thought of the *Pater Noster*, the *Ave Maria*, prayers Mama used to drill into me with devotion, words the nuns in summer camp made us commit to memory. But now they were a faint memory, a blur. Still, I didn't give up, for I knew that God could read my heart.

I knelt there a long while, my head in my hands, aware that my fear of failure had driven me here to seek redemption, forgiveness. I remembered the church I'd run into on my first day of school, and wondered what had really driven me this far. Then I opened the gates of my soul and let the flood of emotions and tears pour out. I let them run their course and wash over me until I felt spent.

A peace came over me.

There was nothing more I could do on my own.

Some nights after I closed shop, I lingered in the kitchen, smelling the scent of baked bread, garlic, and the nutty flavor of fried oil that had seeped into every crack in the ceiling and walls. The stove looked good with a coat of oil bringing back its bygone shine. The four-level wheeled cart stood ready nearby with the ingredients to build each dish from scratch and bring it to completion.

A wooden table sat on the left side of the stove, filled with a pyramid of warm platters. This was the dish-up counter. Above it was an L-shaped steel rack that held four piles of skillets and take-out orders. On the right side of the stove, a metal sleeve hung on its side containing bottles of cooking wine. These objects meant little in themselves. But in unison they became an orchestra, and I never ceased to marvel at how essential each piece became when a flurry of business came along. Over time, they had also become my silent companions, sharing joy, sadness, and long intervals of dreadful silence waiting for customers to come in.

Occasionally, when Mama left early at night, I had dinner alone. My favorite way to eat in my own restaurant was to heap a plate with prosciutto, Parmigiano, olives, plenty of shelled walnuts, and slices of tomatoes with anchovies, accompanied by a crunchy baguette. I complimented it all with a glass or two from Father's private reserve, just to relax my mind. Oh, I needed it, too.

Working alongside Mama all day I sometimes felt as if she sucked the air out of the room. She loomed large over my life, and over everything else. I had given up telling her what to do, or how. Her ways were always better than mine. And when I insisted on something, she offered me heaps of criticism. She always ended up having the last word on every subject.

On these occasions it occurred to me that the dining room was comfortable and charming. The new wooden mint-green, straw-lined chairs gave a cozy Mediterranean ambiance to the place. And the whole place seemed cozy and welcoming as though you were at home. Moreover, Mama was right. A good feeling permeated the air inside the shop—perhaps Mama's numerology theory had some validity. During most mornings, the sun rising from the east flooded the shopping center with its warm rays and coated the shop's walls in rich yellow tones, overshadowing the bleakness of the center. As a result, working in the kitchen was pleasant. It had become a place where I could enjoy each task with deep satisfaction, making my work seem more like play.

Being alone there gave me a chance to brood over business and reflect on my new relationship with Jane. She had infused joy into my life again. The mere thought of her presence colored the drudgery of everyday living and gave it new meaning. Although I was still drawn to her, I could feel the intervening years had changed me. The passion that had once consumed me wasn't as strong anymore. Jane still had a certain streak of stubbornness in her, that sense of independence that's so characteristically part of the American female psyche, and which has always intimidated me, possibly kept me away from re-marrying. Perhaps it was the stress of the business, or the years that had passed. But who knew? Things might get better in time.

One night, Jane helped me to make pasta. No—I made pasta while she watched. She watched as I poured a blend of water and eggs into a funnel to moisten the semolina spinning inside the machine. An expression of discovery and curiosity upon her face. She observed the transformation of the ingredients, the pasta being extruded through the dies, pliable and smooth and golden, and she begged me not to cut it. "Tie me up in it, won't you?" she whispered softly into my ear above the roar of the motor, her throaty voice rising and falling like a melody. It was nearly impossible to deny her anything, let alone such a silly request.

She stood close to me, arms raised in surrender, her body twirling slowly, as I draped her with the warm bundle of strands. "Tie me good. Tie me down," she hummed. As the machine groaned and churned, Jane's eyes were veiled with joy and her hips swayed voluptuously to the rhythm of the blaring music. "Tie me good. Tie me down."

Had Mama seen me, she would have disowned me on the spot.

However, following this act of exhibitionism, my conscious nagged me. Guilt lingered heavy and muffling. Food to me, as to Mama, was sacred. There had been nights when I went to sleep in Calabria on an empty and growling belly. Yet now that I had been blessed to live in the abundance capital of the world, I was playing with food, disrespecting its sanctity. Moreover, making pasta and boiling it were the two rituals that I looked forward to with joy. For they allowed my mind to drift to its farthest corners. Every time I did this, I felt as if I were embarking on a journey, visiting new places, encountering new faces, revisiting old ones. My reveries provided a break from insurance premiums, rent, payroll, and all the other pressing business worries. This was pasta time. Watching water come to a boil, or, if I was making pasta, watching the semolina spin inside the vat, transported me to a world that became still and silent, ready to listen if I had anything to confide. And it was during these blissful moments that I could see things clearly, that the rumbling inside my head would stop, allowing me to reconstruct my life piece by piece. And the marvelous thing was that I could give my full attention to whatever task was at hand while I leisurely strolled down the path of my imagination.

There was a certain tranquility after everyone had gone, and the restaurant would become quiet and safe, like a womb. At last, the day's frantic activities had ceased, and now time itself seemed to be resting and reflecting.

There was music, too. But not from the radio. It was the gentle music of the icemaker, the refrigerator's motors, and the ticking of the green-lined clock on the wall. And there was the livelier music of the crickets that lived under the icemaker. Their chirping was the sign that had convinced me to go ahead with the venture the first time I stepped inside the place. I chuckled now, thinking how delusional I must have been to buy a business based on the presence of crickets on its premises. But Nonna swore crickets brought good luck. And according to my calculations, based on the number of crickets, I should do more than just fine.

I found driving at night liberating after an interminable day at work under the incessant glare of the florescent lights. Many a night, after I closed shop, I would slide into my car, exit onto Bullard, and veer off onto Palm to reach Herndon Avenue, which by now had become a major thoroughfare—three lanes each way—to accommodate the new growth of a town that, along with Bakersfield, was one of the last affordable places in California to buy a home.

With the new freeway 41 that had been built in recent years, and which cut through town, splitting it in half like an orange, Blackstone, once the king of streets, had lost its old allure. Although it was still heavily trafficked at just about all hours of the day, at night, after ten o'clock, something strange seemed to happen there sometimes. As you drove toward downtown, if you looked closely over the dashboard, you could see a thin black veil lifting above its tar surface, which shimmered in the car's lights like a fine mist. It never lifted much higher than a foot or two above ground, as though it wanted to make itself visible, known, heard. I saw it often as I drove during the night. For a long time I was puzzled by it. Then I figured out what it could be. This was the street's soul reemerging above ground as if trying to reclaim its old glory, which once had made it shine with youth's yearnings, loud laughter, and the glow of a full moon. The black mist was no less than the street's silent grieving for the loss of its popularity. And like an old dying king, no one remembered it, no one paid any attention to it anymore.

In comparison, Belmont Avenue had become a true relic. As I drove through it now there was a palpable sadness, as though this part of town had died. The original Di Cicco building, where I had spent countless nights tossing pizza in the air, my back drenched in sweat from the double-decker oven, had now been leveled to make way for the freeway entrance. The Big Boy burger joint south of it was boarded up. The pizzeria on the southwest corner, owned by an Italian family with a bunch of unruly kids that worked the place and chased each other inside, was also gone. And as I drove around the neighborhood now, a heart-wrenching loneliness hovered in the air. A feeling of desolation permeated the area as though no one lived here anymore. What remained were only the faint voices of those warm summer nights flowing inside my head. This was what saddened me about America. There was no past. Everything was in a constant state of flux. Nothing remained the same for long. The old was tossed into the scrap-heap to make way for the new. This created a constant feeling of impermanence. And as everyone longed to move to the suburbs, the abandoned older parts of town crumbled and slowly became sad and lonesome ghosts. This was the dark side of the frenetic beat of America that had seduced me in New York so long ago.

I drove home through the charming old Tower district, with its landmark theater presiding over the neighborhood like a nostalgic dignitary of a bygone era. Its Bohemian ambiance floated in the night air, always managing to lift my spirits.

The night wouldn't feel complete without a quick tour along old Van Ness, with its forest of timber—oaks, pines, and eucalyptus—distributed among the dark, inconspicuous mansions. However, every December this street became Christmas Tree Lane, lighted by millions of multicolored holiday lights intertwined through a half arch-shaped metal wire structure, creating a mosaic of brilliant lights illuminating the night. Then the street and its mansions—which seemed dormant during the year—came alive, boiling with an air of festivity. Some of the homes threw quaint parties. Neighbors and friends convened around crackling fireplaces, amidst loud laughter and a joyous spirit, while tables full of appetizers gleamed under dim lights. And outside, under floating strands of damp and misty fog, carloads of citizens young and old paraded down the magic street of town for the whole month, soaking in the holiday spirit.

Christmas was hiding around the corner, and soon enough it arrived. There was a little flurry of new business due to the holiday spirit. Then it would be back to square one.

Christmas meant goat meat on the table to celebrate the holidays, in keeping with Calabrian tradition—we used a whole goat from Wilbert Meats with all its entrails, lungs, heart, liver, kidneys, which Mama sautéed with onion and wine. It was a delicacy we looked forward to each year. The rest of the meat was usually oven roasted till the meat pulled away from the bone. Heaven, really. And on our table there were never any leftovers, no food ever tossed.

Around the first week of January, Madeline Davidson, a local food critic, mentioned us in her column. Silvio called me from his school to give me the news. She had written only a few lines, he said, but they had been very positive.

I dashed out and bought the day's paper at the stand outside Food Land. With sweating palms, I scanned the pages until I found it. A smile grew on my lips.

A considerable flock of new faces came in that same day. Perhaps Mama was right about the saint always answering her prayers, and Nonna about the luck brought on by crickets.

By the end of February there was a definite increase in business. When I totaled the weekly sales I realized that if the trend continued, I might soon be able to repay my debt. For the first time, I could see light at the end of the tunnel. Excited by these prospects, I hired my first server. An urge rose in me to put my arms around Mama and thank her for her efforts, but I didn't want to get her hopes too high. At least not yet.

GNOCCHI AL GORGONZOLA

GNOCCHI WITH GORGONZOLA

Serves 2

This recipe is dedicated to the memory of my dear friend, father Sergio Negri.

½ lb of gnocchi. They are available at most delicatessens nowadays, or you can make your own.

6-8 oz cream

4 oz Gorgonzola (If unavailable, use good quality blue or Stilton cheese.)

1 tablespoon minced parsley

Salt and pepper to taste

Pour cream into a medium-size skillet, and set over unlit stove.

Bring medium pot of water to a full boil. Add 1 tablespoon of salt, and gnocchi. Place skillet on low heat. Gnocchi are ready when they float to the surface, about 2-3 minutes (check package directions). Drain and add to skillet. Increase flame to medium heat until cream foams. If using blue cheese, crumble it and add it to the cream. If using Gorgonzola, dissolve it into the cream with a spoon. Add salt and pepper to taste. Let cream reduce and coat gnocchi smoothly. Do not quit too soon or it will be watery.

Add parsley and grated Parmigiano. Serve.

TWENTY

At almost equal distance between Los Angeles and San Francisco, in the heart of the Central Valley, lies Fresno. It is a lovely place built on the valley's floor, flat like a table, bordered to the east by the Sierra Nevada mountains, and to the north by Yosemite.

Spring in the San Joaquin Valley is a time of magic. A time when change can be felt in the air. When it arrives in late March or early April, spring brings a soft and lively feel, a sense of renewal, as though life is starting again. The sprouting of new leaves on trees, the blades of mustard greens and colorful flowers all burst forth with untamed vigor and infuse the air with their sweet and pleasant smell.

The doves are busy building their nests with painstaking patience, hauling dry twigs in their clenched beaks, arranging them with infinite care under the rafters of the houses. Father always smiled at the spectacle. Outside town the furrowed fields of young grain protruding inches above the ground shiver and sway in the morning chill. The glittering dew on the branches of apricot trees trembles like tears about to fall. The almond trees are in full bloom, with their mosaic of stunning colors. Their pollen drifts slowly into town, bringing sniffles and tears and misery to a considerable number of Fresno's citizens. The vines along Clovis Avenue are a soothing green, their branches loaded with berries that by August will have swelled into five-pound clusters of sweet white grapes. The Blossom Trail along Jensen Avenue is a brilliant quilt of colors, as though once a year God sees fit to bestow unsurpassed beauty upon this hot, flat stretch of land to reward it for growing most of America's produce. The rolling hills east of Clovis lie fat and luscious like a woman's bosom. The brown and black cattle graze in shallow green grass. And the scent of orange blossoms lingers pungent and sweet in the afternoon air.

In the morning, the patio of the Boulangerie is packed with nodding heads and flapping tongues, as cups touch lips, and anxious fingers tear at sweets. And in the sky, an army of specks of pollen advances toward town, anxious to claim its next victims.

It was with this exhilarating feeling of life beginning anew and confidence born from the critic's article that I threw myself headlong into work. It was a good tonic for my restless nature, and it made the long hours pass quickly.

And who knew. There could be more articles coming along, if only life might decide to cast its favor my way again.

Then in mid-March, along with the quick bursts of rain that left the ground begging for more, came Sabine Morrow. Another critic, she came in, ate, and wrote an overwhelmingly positive review. I still had no clue who these mysterious people were. This time the article was half a page long and lavished high praise on the spicy linguine New Orleans, the succulent gnocchi al Gorgonzola, the rich and creamy polenta, and a few other dishes.

When Sabine came in and introduced herself a few days later, she eyed me as if I were a little mad. "You must have had enormous confidence to think you could get away with serving food on paper plates. And of all places, in this town. Either that or you must be out of your mind. Which one is it?" she asked with glee.

I thought of explaining to her the circumstances that had led to this embarrassing reality. But I knew she would have been bored by the details. "A little of both," I said, chuckling.

I hired five new employees and replaced the plastic silverware. I would change over to plates and wine glasses over time.

Then all hell broke loose.

People invaded the place like the flocks of multicolored birds that had flooded the oak trees of my village in late September as they migrated back to Africa. It was pandemonium. Customers lined up on the sidewalk waiting for the next available table. Inside, the phone rang non-stop. The twenty-seven-seat dining room was packed and loud with talk and laughter. Take-out orders alone were a nightmare. The staff and I, Mama included, scurried around to serve customers like chickens chased by a dog. In the tumultuous rush to survive the invasion, I could hear Mama somewhere in the kitchen cussing in English. *Shet. Sanamibici. Dis no gud.* I giggled, knowing that whatever she was doing, it wasn't going her way.

She also displayed her leadership skill by issuing orders in Italian to a bewildered young kitchen helper—the last recruit—and the young hostess who acted as a go-between. Neither of them should have been able to understand Mama, but amazingly they did, as they followed her instructions with a clear "O.K., O.K." I supposed Mama had some mysterious method of communication I wasn't aware of.

The spindle couldn't hold the flood of tickets. I moved at the stove like the piston of an engine. Skillets flew through my hands. My fingers moved like those of some insane pianist as I built each dish from scratch, dishing out four, six plates at a time.

This was madness.

I couldn't sleep at night because when I closed my eyes I saw tickets, skillets, plates, and curtains of dangling pasta. I remembered the days in Milano delivering with the old bicycle in the rain and snow, and wished my uncle Frank was alive to see me now.

I had made it.

I was jubilant. I sang Italian arias in the back lot. The restaurant looked different, as if I were seeing it for the first time, with new eyes, as though I had changed lenses and the world instantly became renewed. I even smoked in Mama's vicinity without fear of retaliation. She cast me incinerating glances, but didn't seem to care so much now. Perhaps the sweet *ting ting ting* of each transaction of the cash register had shifted Mama's priorities, softened her. My neighboring merchants were proud of the center's new notoriety. Lines of expensive, shiny cars were parked by the curb. Sweet success had arrived. I had been dreaming of this moment for so long. Success felt sweeter, since it came unexpected.

I wondered if it would last.

This grueling pace continued unrelenting for weeks. People came from as far as Tulare County. Everyone knew my name. Total strangers flashed smiles, reached out their hands, and if I was behind the stove, where I was most of the time, they waved like old acquaintances. I felt like a rock star. Everyone wanted a piece of me.

Nancy Osborne, the local television announcer, and her colleague, Mama's all-time favorite local weather anchorman Angelo Stalis, paid us a visit. Mama cast him excited, furtive glances from the kitchen, and nudged me, demanding further confirmation of the man's identity.

I called PGE to see if I could get them to increase their gas output. Trying to keep up with the insane demand, I had increased the stove's burners to maximum capacity.

"What are you trying to do, torch the place?" the service technician said, eyeing me uneasily, examining the tongues of fire leaping up from the burners when he turned the knobs. "You are all maxed out here. Get yourself another stove."

Yeah. Get myself another stove. Easy for him to say. Where would I put it?

Ecstatic with our success, Mama recounted Grandfather's advice: "Place these coins into the baby's hand, close into a fist and hold it for a few seconds, just before you cut his fingernails the first time. It will bring him wealth one day." He had told her this upon his last return from America.

Perhaps my path to America had been laid out long before I was born, and Grandfather's gesture had helped seal that fate. Mama honors his memory to this day by keeping a votive candle lit before his only surviving faded black-and-white photo on the mantle.

In the kitchen, the chopped scallions, minced garlic, diced tomatoes, butter, sliced mushrooms, and the rest of the items were evaporating, swallowed by the flame-crowned skillets. Mama's face was flushed with pleasure and exhaustion. She groaned at the flames that shot into the air, flinched at it, and raised her hand in fear. "*Ma, e' necessariu su vinu?*" Was the wine necessary? I had no time to answer. My adrenaline was pumping, my reflexes alert like a tiger chasing a prey. My brain sped ahead of my body, coordinating each order. My hands moved with a life of their own. Every movement was calculated, smooth, efficient, rushing to catch up with my brain. My body ran like a machine, a robot of precision and speed. Finally, body and soul had become one. I had reached that blissful state where everything seemed to be still, even serene, like the calm surface of a slowly-flowing river. Yet inside I felt on fire, as if running a sprint. I could keep this pace for weeks, months…years, I assumed then. I felt like a mercenary, ready to annihilate my enemy: the orders on the spindle. This was the high, the zone, and the addiction I sought daily. When each little detail went my way, as they did most times, working the line was the most empowering feeling. A feeling you can't mistake for anything else. Possibly similar to what a ship's captain must experience navigating his vessel on high seas.

Scanning the two-hour waiting line one weekend, I asked myself where in hell I would put all the people if this trend continued. I was stuck with a place that was never intended to serve this many people. The whole thing was an improvised operation. Each day I devised new ways to compensate for the lack of space. What other choice did I have? None.

But mine was a very good problem to have.

I recruited Father to help, but he didn't last long. Mama, second in command in the kitchen, quickly lost her patience with his fastidious ways, handed him the push-broom, and shooed him out of the way.

The compliments were coming in loud and clear. People peered inside the kitchen door and offered them to me like gifts—this was the highest reward for me, what made it all worthwhile: knowing that people were satisfied with the meals. It was a great feeling, and the place was loud with noise and full of life. Happiness seeped through every fiber of my body.

I had my share of complaints, too. "Why don't you have meatballs on this menu? You think you are too good for them?" The most memorable: "Hey, buddy. Where the hell is the tomato sauce on this spaghetti?" Or, "Where do you think you are? In Italy? You carry hardly any California wines." This hurt because I valued them myself, but they were a bit too expensive for my place. I smiled politely.

American wines had been going strong in Europe, had even garnered first place since back in the 1976 Paris competition, to the wild bewilderment of the two old kings, France and Italy, who felt they had been dethroned by a young and implausible newcomer from overseas. Europe had taken notice of little Napa. And I suspect that the two kings were frantically convening behind closed doors to devise a new plan to regain the title.

For the next several months, I couldn't wait to get to the restaurant in the morning. My mind composed new specials while I drove, like a musician visualizing scales. There was so much to prepare, so many new faces to meet, stomachs to please. The excitement of the new day was contagious. And as I neared the center on Palm Avenue, there in plain sight lay my little shop, sandwiched between the bank and the nail parlor. I felt good. And the place felt like mine. I could do as I pleased with it, even stay open twenty-four hours a day.

Following the major public stir from the article, Mama began to look at me with an inconspicuous sort of respect, and I liked it. I loved it. Although her facade was as stern as ever, under that veil of pretense and toughness, I could feel her secret admiration for me.

In the kitchen, too tired to sing, Mama whispered in a low monotone of pleasure and longing. *Calabrisella mia... Facimmu amuri...E trullalleru...* Then she muttered, "See, I told you, the saint has always answered my prayers," and grinned with pride. Her shoulders swayed gently to the beat inside her head, and she smiled in triumph.

I was speechless. I walked over to her, reached for her hands, held them in mine, and squeezed them. Then I wrapped my arms around her full waist, planted a kiss on her forehead, and told her that I loved her. A few tears trickled down her face as she forced a little smile, her hand sliding down my cheek.

I was glad I had found the strength to utter those words. For some men these are difficult words to say to a mother. But I've no doubt that they're the sweetest and most precious sounds she'd like to hear.

On Easter Sunday Mama came down with the flu. Lying on the couch in the living room, covered with a blanket, watching television, she handed me a sealed envelope and told me to take it to the eleven o'clock Mass offering. This was her way of thanking the saint for having answered her prayers. I stared at the envelope in my hand. It felt quite bulky. "How much did you put in here, Ma?"

"Never mind. That's none of your business. Just do as I say," she said with a hoarse voice and stuffy nose. "And be careful with your head always floating in the clouds. Make sure you place the envelope right inside the basket. And light a candle to the saint too." Her thin, piercing voice reminded me of Nonna's now.

The timely unfolding of events that had rescued me from the brink of failure now seemed more than a mere coincidence. Maybe my star had been guiding me all along, orchestrating the circumstances of my life and watching my every step like it had on that summer night in Milano years ago.

I cruised on the crest of that wave of popularity for months. Business had more than tripled. And besides Mama and my sister-in-law, six new employees now worked for us. But finding qualified kitchen help proved challenging in the Central Valley. With the demands of my type of cuisine it was particularly difficult, and the fact that I am a stubborn perfectionist didn't help matters.

Then, on a drizzling, overcast morning in late November, when the red and gold leaves fell and the dense gray fog hovered over the valley, word came that Nonna had died. I heard Mama answer the phone in her room. A moment later her wail filled the house.

Mama hobbled, dazed, from one room to the other for days on end, her head slumped, her eyes blank. I wanted to go to Nonna's funeral, but no one else could run the kitchen. I thought of closing for a week to go. But I decided I couldn't stand to see her lying lifeless in a coffin. Growing up, I had envisioned her lasting forever, as if she were made of steel and not flesh. And now all that remained were memories. Memories of when she smiled, lips slightly parted, head tilted sideways. Or the way her eyes lit up with delight when she filled my plate with the biggest portions of food at the dinner table. Or when I used to hide behind her, clasping the soft flesh around her girth, to escape Mama's ire. Or the times when I brushed the soft skin of her face with my hand to thank her for saving me from a good beating, for raising hell with the local priest to get me and my brothers used clothes, shoes. Her love for me defied explanation. Perhaps because I was her first grandchild. Possibly her favorite. That's how I wanted to remember her. I knew she would understand.

One by one, the relatives who had shaped my life were passing. Sometimes their existence seemed only a vague dream. If it weren't for those distant voices we heard over the telephone to remind us a piece of us was still connected to them, we might have forgotten them. The irretrievable past had done its work, filled in the gaps of memory for all of us. With Nonna's passing a whole way of life died for me. Visiting Milano wouldn't ever be the same. She was gone now. Gone forever. Those words Nonna uttered the day she anointed me before departure were the greatest encouragement I'd ever received. "Go. See the world. See it for me, too, *figlio mio*. Don't let life pass you by. Don't let life pass you by." Those words will resonate in my ears for a long time. *Figlia mia* were the same words Nonna had whispered clutching my aunt's hand, leaving this world, exhaling her last breath. Only they were directed at Mama this time, her beloved oldest daughter who in her eyes had abandoned her to move to America, my aunt said.

My father didn't shave for forty-five days. He wore a black cloth button pinned to his shirt in mourning. We might not have been here today if it hadn't been for Nonna's courage to bring us to Milano. I wondered if it was planned to occur this way. Or was it just pure chance? So long, dear Nonna, and say hello to eternity for me. Perhaps we shall meet again one day on the grassy slopes of Paradise, as you used to say.

Mama wrote a poem to be read as a eulogy for Nonna. It was titled "A Mother is Gone." It was ironic that Mama stopped writing after that. She had a stack of poems buried in some drawer that she had written late at night when her restless mind wouldn't settle. She used to read them to me from time to time as we drove around town in my Toyota. I hated listening to them because sometimes I could barely hold back my tears.

Unable to endure seeing Mama devastated by Nonna's passing, I spent all of my time at the restaurant, and some nights I even slept there in an old army cot. This gave me a chance to polish the stove, scrub and shine the floor in the dining room to my standards, and arrange the merchandise in neat, geometric patterns on the shelves. I organized the walk-in, stacked beer bottles on the display shelves, made sure the produce was stowed in its place, retrieved the fragments of clam and mussel shell that had hidden themselves in dark corners, and corrected countless other deficiencies. These were details that would have been taken care of on a daily basis, had I a manager.

I told Mama to take time off. With the new hired help, I was pretty much covered. Besides, helping out for months at the restaurant, Mama had neglected her home chores. Among her favorites was sewing. Most of the fabric shops in town knew her. She would bring her old metric measuring tape and buy the equivalent yards of material. She sewed most of her own skirts and blouses. She could have been a master seamstress with her creative and precise hands. Then there was the garden to supervise, for Father never planted anything without first consulting with her, and of course with the moon. She would tell him how far apart to space the little plants so that as they grew, they could breathe properly and not be crowded. She had an affinity for space and knew how to best utilize it. She also knew the exact moment when to pick fava beans, or *cime di rape*, for instance. Left to his own devices, my father would have left them to wilt on the vine for eternal contemplation's sake.

Occasionally, when she could steady her fluttering mind for a few minutes, Mama scribbled a few old memories from her difficult life. Sometimes she wrote and rewrote a poem several times, struggling for the right words to convey her meaning, to make it rhyme. Little did she know that her love for words had been passed on to me. She always claimed that her life could make a great story, if only she could cajole her mind into putting the words on paper. But a great deal of her time still revolved around the stove, even at home. It seemed that a good deal of her life had been devoted to it.

Whispers were circulating among some of my employees that there were no deficiencies on the premises. It was I who was never pleased. This news stunned me. Maybe the imperfections I saw in my restaurant were nothing more than the distorted projections of my own sick mind. This catapulted me into solitary confinement for a while to reexamine my core values. After a quick reassessment of my belief system, I came back reenergized, like a bear after winter hibernation.

No one said a word. Everyone scattered like startled sparrows, murmuring in surprise as I nailed "Three strikes and you're out" signs to the kitchen walls. I nailed them good, so they wouldn't fall.

Such displays of executive intimidation usually lasted two weeks, or a month tops. And on the cycle went, as my hair turned grayer, my nervous stomach churned, and my panic attacks intensified.

Although I had honest, hard-working employees, many times I felt like the Lone Ranger. Over time I tried all the motivational techniques in my arsenal, from intimidation, which was my most natural tactic, to praise, regrettably my least. And between these two opposite poles, I gained no clue as to the workings of human conduct. Was I wrong to want to unleash the best in each employee? To make them understand that the customer is everything? That without the paying guest there is no business? No paycheck every two weeks? Or was I deluding myself? Fighting a lonely battle?

One thing I was blessed with was not having to worry about my employees stealing. In one form or another, stealing is part of the nature of this business. A couple of plates here, coffee cups there, a six pack of beer, not to mention New York steaks, U10 prawns, filet mignon. Although out of habit I inspected the garbage bins frequently for waste, for excessive scraps of meat, fish, romaine leaves, I never worried about any of my employees stashing dozens of steaks in the dumpster and retrieving them after dark, as I'd experienced elsewhere in the past.

And in the greater scheme of things, my employees all *tried*, some harder than others. And most of them showed up for work. For that I was glad, for a business is dependent on the people running it. If I can be accused of one sin it is that I rarely praised aloud.

It was during one of these preoccupied nights, as I lay on my olive-drab cot in the restaurant, warning the pyramid of baby clams on the overhead shelf not to tumble on my head, that I began to contemplate and jot down ideas for this story, as if to make sense out of life. Only too soon did I realize, with much chagrin, how terrible I'd become with the pen.

The months following Nonna's passing were hard for Mama and I, but the demands of tending the business helped soften the blow. The restaurant gave Mama a chance to make many of her home recipes, which I had never tackled because I can't cook well without measuring ingredients. She always made me crazy with her pinch of this and dash of that. Still, her meatballs became legendary, along with her stuffed peppers and eggplant, beef *braciole*, potato and squash fritters, *pasticcio di zucchine*, and much more. And the fact that she was out of the house socializing and helping in the kitchen filled her with joy, spurred her creativity, and offered her a new challenge every day.

My father rarely came to the restaurant anymore, and when he did, he kept up his vigorous elbow swings in the back lot, as though the whole town needed a good sweep. Father seemed haunted by thoughts of uncleanliness everywhere he looked. Later, he would trudge to the store across the street to try his luck at the lottery—a weekly affair—where he played every possible combination, from birthdays of famous people to dates off random gravestones. But mostly, he stayed home to tend his garden. And what a garden he grew! In late spring his colorful fava bean plants towered over five feet tall. He claimed that his reliance on the moon was the secret of the productivity of his garden. Sometimes he even talked to the little plants as he inspected them with caring eyes and tender hands, as though they were frightened children in need of reassurance. Talking to his plants and washing his hands dozens of times a day seemed strange, but I said nothing because by then I was not far behind him in obsessive quirks. Besides, he was my father. He grew awesome organic vegetables, and I used plenty at the restaurant.

If he hears that I've divulged his secrets, he might not talk to me for a while. But perhaps this is what best sums up an old-fashioned, solitary, stubborn Calabrian man. No wonder they call us *testa dura*, hard-heads. I have no doubt we still hold the world's title in this division.

PROSCIUTTO E MELONE

ITALIAN HAM WITH MELON

Serves 3-4

1 ripe cantaloupe   *Prosciutto, 12-15 slices*

Slice cantaloupe in half. Remove seeds. Cut halves into 1-inch slices. Peel skin beneath each slice except for an inch or so. Arrange slices on a platter. Drape each diagonally with a slice of prosciutto. Serve.

TWENTY-ONE

As a result of the huge splash of popularity generated by the article in March 1992, business increased fivefold. Against Mama's loud protests, I bought my own house on the north end of town after the business settled down.

Some nights, on the way home from work, I parked the car on the edge of the road and walked down to the bluffs of the San Joaquin river. An old-timer client told me that it was once a mighty river crowded with salmon. But the dam had reduced the once-mighty river to a trickle. I sat in the brittle grass above its banks. The sky was riddled with stars and from below the crickets hummed their tunes as the river's faint whisper wafted up to me on the warm night air. And as I stared at the endless sky, I remembered the nights when I sat on the steps of our house in Calabria counting the stars and staring at the darkening mountains. Now I wondered what had become of that little boy I once knew.

Some quiet August nights, when not even a thread of air stirred anywhere across the flat land of the San Joaquin Valley, when a veil of haze hovered below the dome of the pale sky and the heat rose from the ground, I gasped for air in the lingering heat. Many a night I'd drive to some obscure fig orchard to pick and eat figs in the moonlight—so many figs, my heart literally ached to see them become yellow and dried-up on trees in countless yards. I have to confess I ate quite a few off those trees, and even offered them as appetizers wrapped with slices of prosciutto at the restaurant, an alternative to *prosciutto e melone.* Which again, hardly anyone knew.

My relationship with Jane blossomed, then slowly withered away. Fifteen years had changed us. We had grown to see that life isn't a walk in the park, and romance alone cannot sustain a relationship. Understanding, caring, and commitment are also necessary. But for me the latter wasn't there. I'd no mental strength to commit to a woman in the midst of building a business, even if she was the woman to whom I'd once given my heart. Still, Jane remained on my mind.

Running a business is no easy feat. I lived in constant dread that an employee might not show up for work, or that I might lose him to the competition. I hired yet another new kitchen helper, hoping he wouldn't turn out like the others who had come and gone. But soon it became clear he wasn't cut out for this line of work. Speed, coordination, and economy of movement are essential in a line cook. Without this trio, it's nearly impossible to make it in the trenches of a kitchen. A line cook must know the difference in cooking time between chicken gorgonzola, risotto, and *cotolette ai porcini* for the order to come up together, and be able to juggle five, ten, or more orders. It takes enormous coordination of body and mind to bring this off. Then each plate must be garnished properly and wiped clean around the edges before it can go out to the table. It's not only the dish that reaches the table—it's the house reputation as well.

The major article had put us on the map with the rest of the top restaurants in town. It was an honor I cherished, knowing that spot could be snatched away in an instant by some new establishment.

I produced endless specials to stay ahead of the competition and beat the monotony, but some daily repetition at Bella Pasta couldn't be avoided. Any experienced cook will tell you that a lot of success in this business depends on consistency. Each dish on the menu must be prepared in the same fashion every time. One of the biggest problems I encountered in hiring kitchen help was that everyone, especially the people with experience, wanted to do it their own way. This produced chaos until I trained them in my style of cuisine. My motto has always been to promote from within. Start fresh and teach the house style and system.

After countless bodies had come and gone, whether due to poor work ethic or lack of technique and desire, at last I found Octavio. He was fast, coordinated, and punctual, with a great passion to learn—a most important quality. In little over a year he was on the line at my side, his long arms moving with dexterity, even attempting to flip the food in the skillets, breaking into a smile every time he nearly succeeded. And before long I could slow down a bit. It had been almost five years of going full throttle, lunch and dinner, seven days a week. I knew from the start that Octavio would be my disciple.

Those business owners who know this trade well stay vigilant to every little detail that makes this business the wild beast it's known to be. For example, acknowledging customers from the moment they come through the door to the last farewell. But ultimately, to be the talk of the town, the food must be excellent. No fancy presentation, exotic ingredients, or trendy new concoctions are going to save an establishment if the food is lacking in flavor, for although flavor might be subjective, taste buds never lie. This is the kitchen's responsibility, starting with the bread, usually the first item greeting the customer, to the olive oil and balsamic to coat it. Salad, soup, appetizers, and main entrée, all must be perfect. If five or six drops of lemon or balsamic are missing, that vinaigrette dressing is going to be insipid. If a dash of butter in the fettuccine Bolognese is missing, that is another failing. Runny, watery sauces and overcooked veal, chicken, beef, fish, or pasta are not acceptable. And it is a crime to use the same knife you cut chicken with to cut other foods, unless you wash it in between. Serve unwashed greens and you give the customer the taste of sand. A clam that doesn't open spills ocean debris into the sauce. Particles of dirt clinging to mushrooms, scallions, or tomatoes...any of these could lose you a customer. A history of such errors will bring your establishment tumbling down.

I'm not claiming I was perfect. I wasn't. No one can be. But I instilled that working philosophy in all my employees. As a chef and owner, you conduct your own orchestra, your crew. You notice who is lagging behind in the kitchen or at the front of the house, whisk away any dirty plates lingering in front of customers—this distinguishes a fine restaurant from a bad one—lend a hand to that station on the spot, and then fill the next gap. And smile. People don't want to see *a muso lungo* when they go out to eat.

Then tomorrow the sun rises again. Or as my mentor Andrea used to say, "You have to start dirtying all those pans all over again."

I'm still amazed at how such a backbreaking, high-stress profession is glorified by the mass media. I wish some of those critics could spend a day with me in any kitchen, behind hot stoves, shooting flames, slippery floors, and then see what they think at the end of the shift. I'm sure most of them would say, "No, thank you—I think I'll stick to television."

The occasional positive articles continued, and the business reached new heights. We had a total of ten employees. Our popularity kept rising, even with more than half a dozen new restaurants in town.

Food was on my mind every waking moment, even at night lying in bed. I'd go over the following week's specials in my head, thinking what new dishes might lure people in, trying to increase the customer count, and projecting weekly sales.

I monitored the profit and loss statement, eyes keen for adjustments to be made. I strove to get free publicity—the best kind—in any media to generate volume, the lifeblood of this business, to pay off silent partners first: utilities, rent, purveyors, payroll, and insurance.

I was fortunate to have good employees, like Sheryl, the most sought-after server I ever had. And Michael, my first food server who waited on an unexpected full house alone on more than one occasion, scrambling but successful. And with Mama hot on his heels bussing tables and complaining that Americans ate too early, he wondered, "Is *Mamma mia* talking about me?" Armando, my faithful manager, made every customer feel at home with his unpretentious smile. The rest of the hard-working kitchen crew, led by Octavio, became an effective and well-synchronized team.

I pondered the escalating costs of doing business, like the workman's comp insurance, utilities, the rising food costs, or the server that called in sick at the last minute and as a result upset the entire shift. Occasionally I reflected on how my life would have turned out had I not left home, and who I might have been if not a restaurateur.

With business going full throttle, sometimes I complained that we could do more volume if we had a bigger space. Often, when people saw a line at the door, they simply turned away and left. On these occasions Mama was quick to point out that greed was getting the better of me. And it was true. "It's not what you make. It's what you save at the end of the month that counts," she'd warn me, well aware that if I saw a suit I liked, unlike her, I wouldn't think twice about buying it—I had a closet full now. "Some people make so much, yet spend it all. You are close to that bunch, *figlio mio*." Mama knew all there was to know about the art of saving.

But in the greater scheme of things, I couldn't have been happier about the way things turned out. I'm certain that without the critics' reviews I would have failed. And Mama's mystical experience in church remained etched in my mind.

Mama was proud of the business success as well, and although she rarely expressed it openly, keeping up her serious and unyielding facade like a nun, it was written all over the soft contours of her face. And a small flame of joy burned behind her tired eyes.

In 1999, *Bon Appetit*'s Los Angeles branch office contacted me requesting my ragù recipe. "Send it to them," Mama said when I told her, her smile as big as the Calabrian sky on summer nights. I brushed off the idea.

"How many places in town would give anything for a request like that, eh?" she insisted, her eyes gleaming like little blades. I knew this was no ordinary request, and I suppose I should have sent it in just to please her. But we were swamped from another recent review highlighting the risotto, and I never got around to it. Perhaps, subconsciously, I cherished that peculiar Calabrian trait of anonymity.

The nature of this business is such that time slips away at an unbelievable speed. The days swelled into weeks, then months. Years came and went. Boredom crawled into my life. I began to feel the unrelenting beating of time. Sitting outside and watching the mountains, I longed for freedom. The business felt like a chain tied around my ankle. It held me captive and confined to the same dull routine, while the world seemed to be having a great time. The challenge was gone now, no matter how many specials I came up with every day. It occurred to me that I was still plagued with the same restlessness that had driven me away from home in the first place. Gone was the initial spark and excitement of being my own boss, and any notion of expansion. I hoped that the next phase of my life would bring me the contentment I'd been searching for.

In addition, something else bothered me deeply. The exploitation of my fellow men for monetary gain. I knew that was the way of the world, yet my conscience nagged me from time to time. Although I had a natural intuitive sense for business—an essential quality for success—enjoyed its challenges, drew pleasure from devising strategic plans for achieving success, I wasn't nor would I ever be a businessman in the truest sense of the word. I think deep inside me lay a free spirit. A spirit that found momentary peace and joy only when it was shopping at the vegetable market, composing a new special, or trying to string together a decent sentence in my notebook. The act of creation didn't much care how it sprang into existence. It didn't differentiate between a skillet or a pencil; both raised tingling sensations of pleasure in my soul.

Overall, business hadn't turned out to be as fulfilling as I'd anticipated. Cooking and shopping were the most rewarding parts, and, of course, interacting with customers. I kept at it because the business offered me financial and psychological security, but most of all for fear of venturing into the unknown. Although I'd only glimpsed at the complexities of my own mind, I knew I was at heart a simple man: I didn't need thrills and frills.

I felt no different having achieved a certain measure of success now. Maybe others saw me in a different light. But I was the same person. Aside from the satisfaction of a modest accomplishment my life hadn't changed, except that I'd grown wiser about human nature and the enslaving allure of money.

I could also see that the golden years of little family-run businesses like ours were numbered. Corporate fever was spreading at an unprecedented rate, with major chains popping up overnight like *porcini*, taking over huge chunks of the market and bankrupting countless small businesses in the process. One day, as if to prove my assumptions, my major supplier out of Sacramento doubled the minimum weekly delivery requirement. I was already spending hours every week driving to the market, creamery, and Costco (to buy pork, lamb, and ground beef). How was I going to manage now after years of depending on a single supplier? I felt cheated and abandoned, and all in the name of the "bottom line." This surprise sent me scrambling to replace hard-to-find items, like the *mascarpone*, which no one in town carried at that time.

One day I brought up the idea of selling, just to test Mama's reaction. It wasn't the first time I had expressed interest in cashing out. But my parents never believed I would do it. Mama cocked her head, narrowed her eyes, and stared in silence. A stab of pain surged in my chest. Father was a bit more merciful: he got up from the kitchen table and walked out into the garden.

The difficulty wasn't just the decision to sell, but deciding how to sell. Transferring a business is a delicate matter. If word got out too early it could spell disaster. Employees might leave for fear their jobs would be terminated by the new buyer.

The ideal scenario for me was to find a buyer discretely, make the deal, and introduce the staff to the new owner. I'd then turn over keys and responsibilities and simply step out of the limelight. But reality was an entirely different matter.

I agonized for months, my mind in limbo. Was this the right decision? Would I regret it? Would Mama be able to bear the news? This venture had changed her life, given her pride in the community and a sense of purpose and belonging. Selling also meant refueling Mama's faint hope of returning to the old country. Even if this was an illusion, for time had slowly wiped out our past. The place she once called home existed only as a blurred figment of her imagination. Perhaps she'd have nothing to look forward to after this experience.

No doubt though, she would cherish its memories. I hoped she could understand that I had my life to live.

I decided to wait till the end of the millennium, see if the world would still be standing, then sell and move on. Where, I'd no idea. Maybe I was destined to roam the world in search of myself. If that was my path, so be it. In addition, the thought that my life was passing too quickly, and that I wasn't truly living it, agitated me to no end. Although I had no clear notion of what that entailed, the dreadful feeling of not fully sucking the marrow out of life persisted.

I had been successful beyond my expectations only because I had taken a chance, risked everything I had worked for, and never lost hope that my star would light my path. This had been a valuable lesson, to listen to that whisper inside me that had brought me so far from my village. Perhaps it was the silent whisper of God talking to each one of us, as Nonna used to call it as she slid the dark beads of her rosary between her thumb and forefinger with each passing prayer.

There was still plenty of time before the end of the century to get Mama ready. Hopefully I'd find a buyer in the meantime. This, given my standards, would be easier said than done.

One morning just before the end of the millennium, the homeless man packed up his bicycle and left. I never saw him again. Why he had lashed out at me all those years ago, I never knew. No one knows what goes through a man's mind. And if you claim to know, you are usually wrong. I wondered if he would survive the approaching winter, lean and frail as he was. He left behind an eerie emptiness under the rafters where he used to lie. Maybe I felt his absence because deep down I am my brother's keeper.

The millennium came and went. I'd been simmering in doubt, regret, and guilt over what I was about to do. I'd found no suitable buyer. There were a couple of decent prospects, but I wasn't sure that I wanted to sell to either. They both wanted to squeeze blood out of the little place by paying a manager to run it. I detested the idea. I'd feel like a traitor selling our creation to some unscrupulous businessperson who looked at it as purely an investment. I have never liked that insensibility in a person whose most important term was "bottom line."

I'd sell only to someone willing to maintain my high standards, continue the same culinary legacy Mama and I had started. This venture had been like a birth. Mama and I had infused life into the business with our own souls and hands. I wanted to see the place thrive as it had, for the memories were too many, too precious, to see them wash away like rainwater. The little hole in the wall—that's what I used to call it—had become a landmark of sorts in town. I hoped to find a new owner who would commit to keeping it that way.

I thought of the legions of loyal customers. They had become like extended family to me. It was torture to think of abandoning them to the whims of a new operator after

Mama and I had pampered them with sincere food and endless care over the years.

I tried convincing myself that most of them were strangers. Why did I worry as if they were my own children? The customers would be all right with the new owner, if they remained faithful to one another. If not, they would scatter to the wind, and in a month or two Mama and I would be forgotten. And here I was worrying myself sick about them.

I must be nuts.

One day one of my old food servers showed up for lunch. When I told him I intended to sell, he expressed interest in going on his own. He was young, ambitious, and hard working, and I figured why not give him a chance. Besides, he was familiar with the operation. He seemed the perfect choice.

In a few weeks we made the deal. The same day, I went home and delivered the news to my parents. It was the first week of September and the temperatures were still in the nineties. Basil scented the air as my father picked the huge leaves for pesto. Mama was hanging clothes on the lines to dry. Signs of aging were creeping in on them faster now, their hair turning grayer, faces sinking, skin wrinkling.

When I told them I had a buyer, both were stunned. They glanced at one another. Father cast his hazel eyes to the ground, and stared blankly at a row of tomatoes. It was almost the end of the season, and still his plants bore sparse clusters of the red pear-shaped fruits. Father had done a fine job all these years. But now his eyes seemed empty. He was probably wandering the garden of his mind, feeling that his reason to get up every morning was gone. He stood there rooted as if lighting had struck him. Then with great effort he glanced at his watch, trudged past me with an icy indifference, his head down, and disappeared into the garage. Seconds later, I could hear the water hiss inside the pipes, splash on the sink's bottom.

"You're not going to sell the name as well, are you?" Mama asked with pleading eyes. What could I tell her? What explanation could I muster? It was the major selling point. Our whole reputation rode on it. I remembered the countless hours, days, and months we had put into building the business from nothing but sheer determination and love for simple food. The name, that ocean blue sign I kept lit till three in the morning, represented the sum total of who Mama and I were. And with the sale transaction, a part of our lives would be sold as well, vanish. But no words came to my lips. Not a sound.

I stood there unable to move, my soul aching. I'd carried the weight of the world on my shoulders ever since I could remember, and for the first time I wondered who I was living my life for, and whether I had lived it wrong thus far.

Then Mama did something that always tore me up inside. Again, she was crying. Slithering tears rolled down her cheeks, one trembled on her upper lip. I understood the depth of pain I was causing her by selling, by closing a chapter in her life—possibly one of the most important, certainly her most rewarding in terms of discovering that life can have a purpose, expressing her entrepreneurial skill, and contributing to my success. I felt as though something inside her was crumbling, as if her life wouldn't ever be the same. Those years of notoriety in town had come to an end. She'd be cast aside again, slide back into that nebulous immigrant world that would probably never make much sense to her. And I was to blame. But it was too late. Things couldn't be undone, and I knew I had to move on. For each of us must travel his own path, his lonely path.

Soon Mama stepped toward me with clouded eyes, the skin purple and raw beneath her eyes flaming from tears. She wrapped her arms around me and held me tight. She pulled me so close to her, I was momentarily startled. I could hear her muffled sobs and feel the soft quivering of her body. I felt the moisture of her tears run down my neck. But there was warmth, a reassuring maternal affection in that embrace, something which I hadn't experienced since childhood. Then I felt that great motherly love surge again, that unbreakable bond which as an adult you rarely remember anymore.

"If this makes you happy, that's all that matters," she whispered into my ear, amidst sniffles, tears, and half smiles. "Health and happiness can't be bought with money." Then she held me at arm's length, regarded me as if she was seeing me for the first time, wiped her wet eyes with the back of her hand. Her trembling and weary eyes bored into mine. "*Che Dio ti accompagni, figlio mio.*" May God watch over you, my son.

I was stunned. This was the last reaction I had expected from her.

A couple of weeks later, on a Saturday afternoon, I handed the keys to the new owner and wished him good luck.

I lingered by the entrance, my eyes tracing over every inch of the place: the hand-painted mural of the Gulf of Naples on the wall, the porcelain fish a dear friend had given me. "If God doesn't like you, He gives you a restaurant," it said. I chuckled, and walked out.

I sat in my new van in the parking lot and stared at the old wall where I'd sat almost ten years earlier. I dusted the hat of the miniature chef that sat on the seat next to me. I'd taken my dear little friend. I remembered when I left Milano with my brown suitcase, my dreams, and fifty-seven dollars. It all seemed surreal now as I looked at the restaurant with the eyes of a stranger. It was hard to believe I had come this far only to end up staring at that same ugly little wall. Soon a dull sadness hovered over me like a dark cloud. A weight pressed down on my chest, and my throat tightened. Tears of sorrow formed in my eyes. This was my own silent grieving. I envied stoic hearts because I wasn't one. The awareness that I was about to part ways with a dear old friend, to whom I had given the best years of my life, assailed me.

Once the tears dried, I felt a deep sense of liberation. I had enjoyed the simple pleasure of making *pasta al pomodoro*, watching a skillet of risotto come alive with each ladle of chicken stock, brushing a hot focaccia just out of the oven with macerated garlic and oil, and inhaling the titillating aromas of that marriage. I'd always find joy in watching the ingredients in that skillet above the flames transform in an alchemy of colors; tossing pasta into the skillet at exactly the right moment and feeling it absorb the sauce's flavors; adding basil or parsley at the last minute, then flipping it in the air one more time before scooping it onto a warm platter; admiring how naturally it lies mounded in the center and not lumbering all over, buried in sauce. And I'd never forget how my heart thrilled each time one of my creations went out to the customer, and calculating how long it would take for a couple to put aside their differences and get down to the business of eating.

Watching my food's flavor dissipate into the air, get cold, and deflate under the customer's indifferent eyes had always pained me. That, I would not miss. But the rest, I would: the sweet music of the clanging pots and pans echoing in the tiny kitchen, the violent splash of wine hitting the rims of the smoldering skillets, and the sweet fragrance as it evaporated. And finally, the loud, strained sound of my own voice calling, "ORDER UP on table twelve."

In spite of all this, I was now certain that I hadn't been put on this earth to be a restaurateur for life. I was tired of acting as boss, parent, teacher, and referee; tired of interviewing strangers who needed a job just for the money, and tired of staring into their dejected faces as I told them they weren't cut out for this line of work. Maybe another calling awaited me, because it seemed my heart still longed for something more. And it longed no less strongly than it had when I sat on the steps of the little house in Calabria and stared at the snow-capped mountains.

This venture had delivered plenty of ups and downs. But finally I could claim to be one of the very few lucky enough to have made it all the way through a career in this ruthless industry. And had I two or three lives to live, no doubt I'd do it all over again—perhaps a little differently. Mine had been a thrilling ride. I'd accomplished more with eleven hundred square feet and a six-burner stove than most dare dream.

I would continue writing about the experience, for I'd learned much about people, life, and myself. I learned to listen to that little voice whispering inside my head, and that ultimately dreams make us. Most importantly, I learned to believe in myself and never to be afraid to take a chance.

The sun was sinking in the sky with swirls of pink and gold. I remembered the warm summer evenings in Calabria, the feel of the fresh breeze stroking my face, my hair, as I sat on the doorstep daydreaming. A light breeze brought forth by the distant winds of the Scirocco, cool and soothing as it traveled the great distances over the sea, in the calm and starlit night. I wiped my eyes with the palms of my hands, and a whiff of fresh garlic trailed into the air like a memory.

I caught sight of my eyes in the rearview mirror. The lines aging them were more pronounced now. Dark circles framed them. The skin under the sockets was puffed and sagging, inflamed from bending over steaming pots, high flames. I regarded them for a long time, trying to understand who I had become, who hid inside that slender mass of flesh. But there was no denying it. Those were still the eyes of the little boy on the poplar tree looking at the crystalline sea, the mountains, and the red rooftops of the houses below. Home! My heart fluttered, tightened. Home seemed a lifetime away now. And perhaps some of us can never return to it. But although the luster of youth in those hazel eyes had gone, there was still a glow in them—a glow kindled by desire, and the same spirit of adventure that had made me the man I was today. The face in the mirror smiled. We winked at each other.

Like all things, this venture had come to its end. But this was not a sad departure. It was a new, bright beginning, full of hope and resolve. Something better was waiting for me out in the world. It was time to move on in search of a new endeavor, explore new horizons, and call Jane.

I thought about the moment I'd set foot on this continent, those gates I'd eyed with wonder as I entered this new world full of undiscovered promises. Would I spend the rest of my days wishing I could have lived two lives at once? Wondering whether if it hadn't been for Al, I might have turned out to be someone other than who I'd become? But the ultimate question was this: Would I do it all over again?

Yes.

I glanced at the restaurant. Twilight was fast settling in. There was a melancholy beauty to it now. Soon the restaurant's lights would glow, announcing the passing of another day. Then, when the last diners had gone and the new owner had closed, a pool of shadows would spill out onto the sidewalk. And in the obscurity and quiet of the unfolding night, a part of me would linger forever.

So long, dear friend.

I started the engine and drove away.

LINGUINE NEW ORLEANS

Serves 4

1 lb linguine.   Cook pasta as per previous recipes.

2 tablespoons olive oil

10 oz sliced mushroom of your choice

1½ tablespoon minced garlic

6-8 oz diced ripe tomatoes

4 oz marinara sauce

30-35 41/50 prawns

2 oz clam juice

Tabasco, Worchester sauce, salt and black pepper to taste.

1 tablespoon minced parsley.

Peel, and pat prawns dry.

In a large skillet, sauté mushrooms in oil for three to four minutes. Add garlic. Follow with tomatoes. Salt and pepper. Let it simmer for about two minutes. Add marinara sauce and clam juice. Simmer for another minute. Add prawns and almost immediately follow with cooked pasta. Toss well for about a minute. Add Worchester sauce, Tabasco, a sprinkle of oil and parsley. Serve.

APPENDIX 1:

Suggestions for cooking pasta.

- Always use a tall pot with plenty of water. For one pound of pasta—fresh or dry—use approximately 5 quarts of water.
- When the water comes to a full boil, add a tablespoon of salt, then immediately add the pasta. Cover the pot and bring water back to a boil. Then remove lid.
- Stir the pasta with a long wooden spoon as it cooks. This keeps pasta from sticking together, provided you have plenty of water in the pot. Be careful; boiling water spits back.
- Cooking time varies according to the shape, size, and type of pasta. Fresh pasta cooks faster than dry pasta. Check package cooking instructions, but always taste.
- Pasta should be cooked until it is tender but firm to the bite, or *al dente.*
- Once pasta is cooked, drain it, then transfer it to a skillet or pot of waiting sauce. Toss.
- Never wash pasta. The only time pasta is immersed in ice water to cool and stop further cooking is when making lasagna, cannelloni, or manicotti.

APPENDIX 2:

Basic marinara sauce.

- 32 oz Italian plum tomatoes with juice. Puree in blender.
- 1 medium white onion, finely chopped
- 1 clove of garlic, minced
- 2 tablespoons olive oil
- 1 teaspoon salt

In a medium-sized pot over low heat, cook onion in oil until translucent, 5 to 6 minutes. Add garlic and stir until golden. Add tomatoes and juice. Salt. Allow sauce to come to a boil. Simmer and reduce for about 30-35 minutes. Stir frequently. Sauce is done when it has reached a nice medium-thick consistency.

The first picture of my mother and me